A Book of Honey

János
Rudnay
László
Beliczay

A Book of Honey

Its history and use

Corvina

Title of the original: Mézkönyv, Corvina Kiadó, 1987
Translated by Inez Kemenes
Translation revised by Marion Smith

The colour photographs showing the life of bees were taken and are reproduced here by courtesy of Donat Waltenberger, Mindelheim, Bavaria
Black and white photographs by Melitta Bach, Zsuzsa Erdőkürti, István Horváth, Ilona F. Molnár, László Szelényi, Péter Varga
Design by Erika Urai

Contents

What Is Honey?

Honey is one of mankind's most ancient nutriments. It has been consumed together with meat, milk, plants and various seeds, since time immemorial. Cavemen probably became familiar with honey very early on, but only legends and myths remain of the time and circumstances of its discovery.

What actually is honey?

Honeybees collect nectar from flowers or the sweet fluid on the leaves, shoots and twigs of plants. Then, mixing this with secretions from their glands, transform it and, after depositing it in the comb, ripen it into honey.

Honey is primarily of vegetable origin. Its sugars are formed in plants by the sun, from water and the carbon dioxide in the air. Its minerals come from the soil through the sap; its proteins are primarily amino acids of plant origin. Its enzymes, and its hormones and vitamins are of vegetable and animal origin.

Bees transform the saccharose of the nectar into honey and invert sugar with the help of enzymes and acids, causing the evaporation of much of its water content at the same time. Transformation goes on during storage—this is why honey is considered a "living substance".

The Swedish natural scientist Carl von Linné classified the bee as *Apis mellifera* (collector of honey) in his taxonomy of animals, but later renamed it *Apis mellifica* (honey maker) when he realized that the bee's role in producing honey was more significant than he had previously thought. The former name is used in the USSR and the USA, whereas in most European countries, including Hungary, the *mellifica* version is accepted.

The bee is a domestic creature but very different from others belonging to this category. You cannot talk to it as to a horse or a donkey, you cannot stroke it or praise it as you can a cow or a dog. Bees are not man's personal friends as cats, goats or lambs may be. They can hardly be altered genetically, unlike Hungarian sheep dogs, basset hounds, St. Bernard dogs or poultry, to mention but a few. Even for the beekeeper, a bee is more of a peculiar object than a pet, it has no emotional ties with its owner. We can care for it, or rather for them, but a bee is not a "creature with a soul", we do not grow of it as of an individual; bees are only of help to man.

Man prepares a home for his bees, constructs a drinking place for them and even provides them with food, but cannot hand-feed them or offer them a drink, nor can he educate them or change their habits. Bees need not be urged to work, they will labour assiduously without prompting. What man can do is to provide the right conditions.

Bees' produce:

—Honey, which was the reason for the domestication of the bee, as it meets a constant human need for food.

—Beeswax, which in the form of candles has provided several generations with light.

—Pollen, which dried at 40 °C and preserved in carbon dioxide, has become a nutrient in the last sixty years.

—Propolis, which when removed from the hive and dissolved in alcohol, has antiseptic and analgesic effects. Applied under a plaster it will eliminate boils, swellings, insect bites and the pain caused by them.

—Bee poison, which is used to alleviate arthritic, especially rheumatic pains.

—Royal jelly, the food supplied by worker bees for the queen bee. It is a very important roborant for children, old people, convalescents and mothers-to-be.

The discovery of honey

Hymenoptera appeared on the earth about 40 to 50 million years ago together with flowering plants. The first traces of bees belonging to the *apis* species were found in Europe, embedded in amber at Holzminden in the Riesengebirge.

It took about 200,000 years for our anthropoid ancestors, who appeared about 400,000 years ago, to learn to speak and use tools. It was about 30 to 40 thousand years ago, in the neolithic age—at about the same time as they discovered fire—that they turned from primitive hordes, gathering plants for their livelihood, into hunters. In the meantime, they observed that from certain hollow trees and crevices in rocks, honey was trickling down in the warm sunshine, and they soon came to like its sweet taste. They could also see animals robbing bees' nests and following in their wake, found the coveted sweet stuff. It is not impossible that their attention was attracted by wild bees buzzing around. Initially the bees may have covered the sweet-toothed cavemen and, with their stings, compelled them to flee—though they could probably have done little harm to their hairy, weather-beaten skin. Primitive man finally realized that bees, if kept alive, would continuously supply him with honey. He marked the tree with the bees' nest and returned from time to time to take away a few combs of honey. Ten to fifteen thousand years ago man did not only satisfy his immediate hunger, but also built up reserves of food. A moment of this activity is represented in the pictograph discovered in 1919 in Spain, in the Spider Caves (Cuevas da la Arena) hidden in the mountains, north-east of the village of Bicorp in Valencia. In the drawing a man is climbing upwards with the help of clinging roots and the vines of some creepers hanging from a wall of rock. His companion has already reached the crevice in the rock in which a colony of bees was living. The hunter in front of the bees' nest holds a basket, coated with clay, in his hand. There are bees flying all around him ready to defend their store of honey. A similar container can be seen on the back of the climbing man. Around the entrance to the bees' nest something seems to be swirling. It is conceivable that smoke was used even as early as this to overpower the bees.

Even before the discovery of the Bicorp pictographs, rock paintings of honey collecting were found in the north of Spain and in the Lascau Caves (south-western France), and then, later, in Northern and Eastern Europe, as well as in Asia and Africa.

It was probably in the eighth–seventh centuries B.C. in southern Anatolia and the neighbouring valley of the rivers Tigris and Euphrates, that nomadic tribes of hunters changed over from gathering seeds to sowing seeds and tilling the land. Settling down made it possible to locate already known bees near to the permanent dwelling places of man in man-made "bee-houses": holes hewn into rocks, hollow trees and perhaps in basketwork skeps. The drying and baking of clay vessels became familiar between 6500 and 5500 B.C. so that pots fit for keeping and storing honey were already available. Honey became one of man's basic nutrients.

Written Records and Historical Evidence of Bees and Honey

There is not much information concerning early uses of honey in the Far East. One of the oldest pieces of evidence is the medical work which was written in China in 2700 B.C. entitled Nu-tsi-kiang, disclosing the secret of longevity. One of the author's prescriptions is the regular consumption of pulverized ginseng root mixed with honey. The wisdom of this advice has since been confirmed by scientific research all over the world.

According to the description of Strabo (68 B.C.–A.D. 19), author of *Geography,* the Indus valley was very rich in honey. This is confirmed by old Sanskrit sources: the *Vedas,* the sacred books of India, written in about 2000 B.C. make mention of bees *(madhukarika)* and of honey *(madhu).* Madhu is also the name given to a legendary giant, two kings and several families and villages—an obvious sign of the importance of honey.

According to legend, in the days of King Vikramaditja—who ruled for three hundred and one years—there were so many bees in the Vindhya mountains that Lakshmi, the goddess of good fortune and wealth, also ruled over the bees. Large quantities of honey came from the legendary Himeret mountains, where jasmine, mangoes, *madhuka* and different varieties of lotus were in blossom all the year around.

As early as the time of Manu (2nd century A.D.), some kind of sugary juice was made of cane, but honey was much more highly valued. Of the latter, a certain proportion had to be delivered to the king. The superior value of honey was later confirmed by Pliny the Elder (A.D. 23–79) the Roman author, in his works on natural history, and by Dioscorides in his *De Materia Medica.* Dioscorides Pedanius was a military surgeon of Greek origin in Rome, in the first century A.D. As a botanist and pharmacologist he was an authority referred to as late as the Middle Ages.

In India, priests and soldiers were forbidden to trade in honey; there were merchants specializing in this product. According to the *Vedas,* people believed that life in the next world is made even more pleasant by the humming of bees.

According to Zoroaster (7th century B.C.) of southern Persia, Persians had no knowledge of bee-keeping; they robbed wild bees of their honey. The *Avesta*, their holy book, written in the first millennium B.C. describes a wedding

Maltese coin with bee cells, bee and dolphins. 1972

to which the bride arrived from a foreign country. The duties of the servants escorting her, and herding her dowry of animals, included the collection of honey on the way to Persia for the wedding.

Honey was also used as a medicine and for sacrifice. We also know of people condemned to death, who were tied to a stake under the scorching sun, with their faces covered in honey, so that insects attracted by its scent would torture them until they died.

We have some information about bee-keeping in Assyria from the clay tablets in cuneiform script, excavated from the ruins of Nippur (Ni=god, pur=dwelling), and dating back to about 750 B.C. One of their goddesses was even named Mylitta, which means little bee. Bees were also used for military purposes. In the battles during Assyria's wars of conquest, the warriors threw whole hives at the enemy to create panic. In the eighth century B.C. the prophet Isaiah threatened King Ahaz of Judea with the bees of Assyria for flirting with the pagans. And Pliny ranked Assyria among the provinces which gave the largest amounts of honey to the Roman Empire.

Bee-keeping was also important in Egypt. In the southern part of the great temple in Karnak, a pictorial representation of bees, dating from about 1500 B.C. was found in the relief showing King Horus advancing towards Amon. There are also bees on the tablet reporting Shnofru's victory. On a tombstone in Thebes there is a quite recognizable hive; what we do not know is whether a bee-keeper or a basket weaver has his eternal rest in the tomb. Obelisks and papyrus rolls, two or three thousand years of age, also contain references to bees.

The assumption that honey processing must also have been fairly advanced in Ancient Egypt, was borne out by findings in pyramids giving evidence of the use of honey and honeycakes.

The French consul, B. Maillot described in his eighteenth-century work entitled *Description de l'Egypte,* that as early as the times of the pharaohs, migratory bee-keeping was known. The hives were put on rafts at the upper stretch of the Nile and floated downstream to Alexandria. They covered such a distance each night that the bees found new pastures in the meadows the next morning.

The use of beeswax in Egypt dates back to mythical times. As legend has it, Isis had the body of her divine husband Osiris cut into fourteen pieces and dipped into spicy wax. According to other myths she had his limbs sculpted out of wax and sent to fourteen provinces of the empire so that people would pray in front of them. The art of embalming was a closely guarded secret, pursued in remote places by doctors, under the supervision of priests.

Of all ancient cultures we know most about the apiculture of the Jews, thanks first of all to the Old Testament. The Jews left Khaldea in the southern part of Mesopotamia, where bees were kept as early as around 2000 B.C. Jacob sent his sons to the Egyptian governor to buy corn for the starving Jews. Is is described in the First Book of Moses as follows:

"And their father Israel said unto them, If it must be so now, do this; take of the best fruits in the land in your vessels, and carry down the man a present, a little balm, and a little honey, spices and myrrh, nuts and almonds" (Genesis 43:11).

The historian Josephus Flavius (A.D. 38 or 39–100) reports that at the time of the Pharaoh Tuthmoses, in the sixteenth–fifteenth century B.C. there was an abundance of honey in Egypt. In the fourth century B.C. the Jews fleeing from Egypt, the "house of bondage", complained to Moses that he had taken them out of the country flowing with milk and honey.

"Is it a small thing that thou hast brought us up out of a land that floweth with milk and honey, to kill us in the wilderness, except thou make thyself altogether a prince over us?" (Numbers 16:13)

The first mention of Canaan flowing with milk and honey is also made in those parts of the Old Testament describing the flight from Egypt; it was the Promised Land in whose description the voice of God called from the burning bush on Mount Horeb, comforting the tired people wandering in the wilderness.

It was during their stay in Egypt that the Jews acquired the methods of bee-keeping prevalent there, and so after they settled down in the land of Israel, in addition to a flourishing agriculture, apiculture became an additional source of income. It is also confirmed by Josephus Flavius in his work *The Jewish War*. The priests collected taxes on bees and ransoms could also be paid in honey.

During their captivity in Babylon (8th–6th centuries B.C.) the Jews acquired further experience in bee-keeping, and when they were able to return to Israel they practised it on such a high level that they sold their honey and wax through the major ports of the Mediterranean.

Although insects were considered unclean, bees were considered an exception because they collected honey from flowers, and it was believed that they created their descendants from flowers too. The Jews thought that the biggest bee in the hive, the queen, was male. Otherwise they made several useful observations in connection with bee-keeping still considered valid today. We can read in the Old Testament of how to tend bees in the winter and during the summer and how to protect them from sunshine and rain; of hives woven from straw and reeds, of swarming and the preparation of wax. The use of the smoker, the pipe, is also described, as well as methods of straining honey and performing other tasks. It also contains legal prescriptions:

—the hives are to be located outside the city wall at a distance of at least fifty ells;

—in respect of the ownership of a swarm, the evidence of women and children can also be accepted;

—the owner is entitled to take his swarm home, even from a foreign land, but when he abandons looking for his swarm he also abandons his right of ownership.

These regulations were in force as early as in Joshua's time (9th–8th centuries B.C.).

Honey was considered the symbol of abundance by the Jews. The mouths of newborn infants were smeared with butter and honey so that their lives would be good and rich. Honey was also thought to be an aphrodisiac.

> "Thy lips, O my spouse, drop as the honeycomb:
> honey and milk are under thy tongue; and the smell of thy garments is like the smell of
> Lebanon." (Song of Solomon 4:11)

> "I am come into my garden my sister, my spouse:
> I have gathered my myrrh with my spice; I have
> eaten my honeycomb with my honey; I have drunk
> my wine with my milk: eat O friends; drink, yea,
> drink abundantly, O beloved."
> (Song of Solomon 5:1)

The Old Testament mentions more than one corpse preserved in honey. Aristobulus' body was carried home to Judaea in honey when, after fighting in Egypt, he was poisoned on his way home. King Herod kept his wife Marianna in a tub of honey for seven years after her death to keep her beauty intact.

This peculiar way of embalming was also

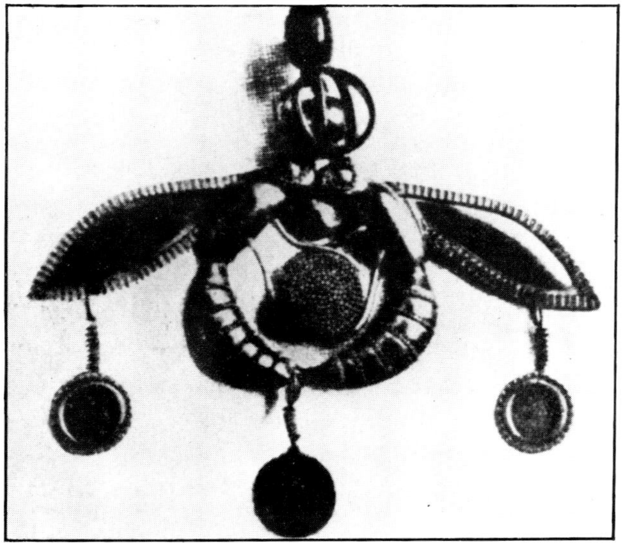

Ancient Cretan gold pendant representing bees, dating from 2000 B.C. Archaeological Institute, Göttingen

known in ancient Greece. Agripolytos, King of Sparta, was taken home in a barrel of honey after he had fallen in battle.

Heinrich Schliemann found, during his excavation of Troy (1870–78), 2900-year-old remains of skin preserved in honey and wax.

In Greek mythology the term *melissa* (honey) can be traced back to the name of the Cretan King Melissus's daughter. It is more likely however, that they had taken it over from Mesopotamian or Egyptian sources.

Homer, whose blindness was thought by his contemporaries to be the result of bee-stings referred to honey in his Iliad and Odyssey as the gift of the gods.

The aging Democritus (5th century B.C.) extended his life, at the request of his daughters, by consuming honey, and as legend has it, died only at the age of 109. As a philosopher he professed that the body must be nourished with honey inside and by oil outside.

The great mathematician Pythagoras (*c.* 570–500 B.C.) and his disciples, lived mostly on bread and honey because he believed that honey had an effect on clearing thought.

Honey was offered as sacrifice to household gods as well as to the goddess of sun and peace, Elmione. The evil spirits of the nether world were also appeased by honey, so they poured honey over the sacrificial food.

The funeral pyre of Patroclus and Achilles who had fallen in the Trojan War, was surrounded by amphorae filled with honey which were then emptied over the ashes.

According to legend, Daedalus and Icarus fled from captivity in Crete on wings made of feathers, fastened to each other with wax; but they flew too close to the sun, the wax melted and they fell into the sea.

In the first century B.C. the historian Diodorus Siculus described that Aristaeus of Kheros had learned hive-making and the hewing of the hive stones in which bees were kept in Attica, from the nymphs.

In the course of his excavations at a Trojan site, Schliemann found clay pots which had been used for emptying honeycombs taken from the hives.

In the days of Pericles (5th century B.C.), 20,000 bee colonies were kept per 2500 hectares, i.e. about eight colonies per hectare. Migrating bee-keepers moved their hives to the Cyclades surrounding the sacred island Delos, as well as to Attica and Euboea.

Aristotle devoted one of his books written on nature, to bees.

Curtius Rufus mentions in his book on Alexander the Great, that in those times an amphora—full of honey—(*c.* 40 kilos) cost 390 denarii, whereas the price of the same amount of wine was 300 denarii. Incidentally, the body of Alexander the Great was also wrapped in cambric soaked in honey in an attempt to preserve it.

It is characteristic of the lasting quality of honey, that some found in the amphorae among the ruins of an ancient Greek temple in Paestum near Naples, was still enjoyable, though considered to be at least 2500 years old.

Bees were kept in Italy as early as during the reign of Numa Pompilius (8th century B.C.), but larger quantities of honey were only produced in the imperial period.

Pliny relates that in the days of Augustus, bees already belonged to the manors. According to Marcus Terentius Varro (116–27? B.C.) in the Via Sacra in Rome bee-keepers had a separate market-place. The hives made for sale were coated with clay or lime but bee-dwellings of baked clay *(alvearia fictilla)* and hives of the same material *(alvearia lactoricia)* were also available. It is remarkable that the same types of hives continued in use up to the end of the eighteenth century.

Pliny advised people only to approach bees when they had washed themselves thoroughly, and not to use any scent, otherwise the bees would most probably attack them.

According to Columella, who lived in the first century A.D., visiting bees must be preceded by preparations observing even more rigorous rules: in the preceding three days it is forbidden to make love, one should beware of getting drunk, a thorough cleansing of the body is advisable and one should refrain from eating strongly salted and spiced foods, especially garlic.

Columella also described that people in the Po valley had learned the craft of bee-keeping so well that they could strengthen weak colonies with brood combs taken from other hives. (In brood combs, still covered larvae are in the process of developing into bees.) The bee-keepers of Hostilia migrated by water with their bees, very much like their Egyptian counterparts had done. When the meadows had been scythed or had withered during an extreme drought, the bee-keepers put their hives on boats at night, and left for better pastures.

Roman chariot of war. Cake mould
from the Pacatus workshop. Second century A.D.
Aquincum Museum, Budapest

We also know that both Aristomakhos and Tasios of Solis wrote scientific works about bee-keeping. The books got lost, but many later authors referred to them.

In ancient Rome apiculture belonged to general culture. It was discussed not only by natural scientists and geographers like Pliny, Strabo and Varro, but also by poets and historians, like Livy, Virgil and Ovid who in his *Ars Amatoria* referred to honey as an aphrodisiac.

Some consuls constructed hives with transparent sides so that they could observe the behaviour and the unceasingly busy activity of the bees.

Sacrificial foods for Sylvanus, the god of woods, Ceres, the goddess of growing vegetation, and Bacchus, the god of wine, were prepared with oil, milk and wine, and honey was poured on top of them. Such dishes were called *meletittae*.

Honey was poured on the threshold of the houses of newly-weds so that their lives would be sweet.

As Virgil sang of it, Aeneas gave honey-cakes to Cerberus—the three-headed watch-dog guarding the entrance to Hades—to eat, so that Charon would take him across the river Styx to his beloved Dido.

Where the bees collected honey from poisonous flowers, people kept them for producing beeswax. In ancient Rome, wax tablets were used instead of paper and writing slates. Wax was used for making candles and torches, for coating wooden vessels and piles to be driven into the ground, as well as for the water-proofing of boats and the walls of baths. The moulding in wax of celebrities, both living and dead, was customary. Also the little statues of ancestors and household gods (*lares* and *penates*) of poorer families, were made of wax. In temples often small lambs and pigs of wax were sacrificed (Cicero: *De nature deorum*).

Bee-keeping, native or imported, also flourished in the provinces of the Roman Empire. In the days of Strabo, the Greek settlers of Gallia prepared embossed earthenware moulds in which honeycakes were baked. In the same area, Egyptian honey amphorae were excavated on the seashore. According to Livy, the island of Corsica paid 200,000 pounds of beeswax as tribute money to Rome.

It is characteristic of the profitability of bee-keeping that the Vaianus brothers, who were soldiers in Hispania in the first century B.C. and kept bees on a territory of one *jugerum* (land which can be ploughed within a day with one team), had a yearly income of 10,000 *sestertii*.

According to tradition, it was the legendary prince of the Celtibers, the autochthonous inhabitants of Hispania, who introduced apiculture in the region. Trogus Pompeius, who lived in the first century B.C. and who was a contemporary of Augustus, informs us that honey was so abundant in Hispania that this country alone could have supplied the whole of Italy. In his book entitled *Historia naturalis,* Pliny describes how the hives were carried uphill by mules to where even in the height of summer there were lots of flowers, so as to increase the production of honey.

Before proceeding to the relevant stories from the Middle Ages, let us give, as a taste of Roman pleasure, a few recipes from an old codex kept in the Vatican.

Assaturam: salt well any kind of freshly baked meat, pour on honey and serve.

Tiropatium: add a little honey and whole raw eggs to a pot of milk, using five eggs for half a litre. Bake in a slow oven and season with pepper to serve.

Dulcia domestica: season pitted dates with walnut kernels, juniper seed or pepper, and cook in honey.

We know from Seneca that Apicius, a rich Roman, was a famous gourmet. He was worth about 10 million *sestertii* so he could afford to spend a lot of time on cooking and inventing meals. His two cookery books were known in Italy in his lifetime, and later in several other countries too. We still have a codex in which the Benedictine monks in Tours (France) put down the recipes of Apicius in 850. The above dishes were quoted from this source.

Large-scale bee-keeping, which started in the centuries of the Roman Empire, continued to flourish under the Meroving dynasty. When the tomb of King Childerich I, who had died in 481, was excavated in Tournay in the sixteenth century, three hundred bees, made of gold, were found ornamenting the robe of the dead ruler. (Chiflet: *Anastasia Childerici regis Anvers,* 1655.)

Bee-keeping in the Monte Casino monastery. Illustration in a ninth-century manuscript kept in the Vatican Museum. (Published by David Knowles in his work *Christian Monasticism*)

King Charles the Great of the Karoling dynasty, who defeated the Avars, had such a large apiary that it brought him a yearly income of 4000 gold coins.

Under the harsh climatic conditions of northern Europe, honey assumed a special significance. In Denmark clay vessels of about 3500 years old, dating back to the dawn of the Bronze Age, were found together with the remains of honey collected from linden flowers. According to the *Eddas,* bees collected honey from the dew falling from the branches of the holy ash-tree, the Yggdrasill.

Queen Elizabeth of England (1533–1603) personally inspected the preparation of mead for her royal household as, lacking vineyards, this was the noblest drink they could produce.

In the Caucasian mountains, which today form part of the USSR, the deities Zozim and Austeya protected the bees before Christianity. People believed it was Svyatoslav, whom they represented by a cornucopia, who introduced bee-keeping thus bringing richness to the country.

We know from the accounts of Bishop Nestor that substantial quantities of honey and wax were traded between Kiev and the Byzantine Empire in the tenth century. Wax production was especially stimulated by the specifications of the Greek Orthodox Church concerning the number of pure beeswax candles to be burnt in churches.

It was presumably in Russia in the fourteenth century that people discovered the method for rearing queen bees. This was a very important step, as a colony without a queen will inevitably die out, as the queen ensures the continuing existence of the bee colony by laying 1500–3000 eggs every day.

It was the great land owner Propokovich, who gave a boost to apiculture at the end of the eighteenth century. He had 2800 hives that he had designed himself and, supported by the state, founded a school for bee-keepers in Palchiki in 1828. (A similar school was established by the Hapsburg Queen Maria Theresa in Vienna.)

Initially German tribes knew only of the collection of wild honey, which they processed into alcoholic drinks. More than one mention is made of this in the *Nibelungenlied.*

We know from I. G. Bessler, who collected proverbs and legends in connection with bees at parish feasts and in market-places at the end of the nineteenth century, that heathen Germans believed that the Valkyries offered mead in gold cups to the slain heroes of the other world in Valhalla.

Tacitus also referred to the merry, intoxicated Germans drinking fermented hydromel in his *De moribus germanorum.* (Hydromel is a mixture of honey and water.)

Already in the seventh century the Germans kept bees in hives and also used them in war. E.g. when, in the tenth century, Emperor Henry I was attacked by his subject the Prince of Lotharingia, hives were thrown among the cavalry. The bees stung the horses, got under the heavy armour and caused such pandemonium that the attackers fled in disarray. More than seven hundred years later when the Swedes laid siege to Kissingen in 1646, the Germans used the same tactics to defend themselves.

In the thirteenth century, petty criminals were smeared with honey and, after being rolled in goose feathers, were put on public display. The poisoning of foreign bees or the adulteration of honey was considered a grave crime punishable by the cutting off of the offender's hand or, quite often, by death. Four hundred years ago this law was still operative in Saxony.

Decrees and statutory rules went into even more detail in Germany in the fourteenth century. It was laid down for example, that an unmarked nest of wild bees could freely be taken possession of. Legal provisions described the course of action to be taken when the bees settled in foreign territory, and to whom the absconded swarm belonged.

Charles IV (1346–68) supported bee-keepers. Apiaries under 10 colonies were not taxed and a special court *(Zeidlergericht)* was set up to settle disputes in connection with bees. Honey and beeswax were free of duty all over the Holy Roman Empire. A note, characteristic of the value of bees, can be found in one of the paragraphs of the *Zeidlergericht*. The value of the 5 hives in the estate of the deceased Michael Coler was estimated at 15 florins, whereas that of 5 cows, 2 oxen and cart was put at 45 florins. That is, two bee colonies were worth almost as much as a cow.

In his book about old legal oddities (*Deutsche Rechtsalterthümer,* 2nd edition, Göttingen, 1854) J. Grimm describes that a jug of mead had to be placed in front of the aldermen when they convened to administer the law. The jug had to be full so that a fly landing on its brim could drink from it.

Tokens of gratitude to the guilds for qualifying apprentices as journeymen, had to be paid in wax, and before the new journeymen left, a feast was held for which the mead was paid for by the lads, while the rest was provided by the master craftsmen.

It was a favourite method of the Inquisition to dip the shirt of the man suspected of heresy in wax and light it, subjecting him in this way to the so-called ordeal by fire, supposing that God would save him if he were innocent. Sometimes people condemned to death were led to the stake in waxed shirts.

When collecting taxes, royal commissioners often required payment in wax for their services; fines and other punishments could also be paid in beeswax.

In the fourteenth century, bee-keepers founded associations in Nuremberg, Lausitz and Frankfurt for the protection of their rights. The one in Lausitz was still operative in the eighteenth century disseminating professional knowledge and experience among its members.

It is evident of the advanced state of apiculture in Germany, that the first trade journal for bee-keepers, the *Monatsblatt für die gesamte Bienenzucht,* was published there from 1838 to 1845. It was followed, between 1845 and 1900, by the prestigious *Bienenzucht*. It was in the latter that publications by the father of German apiculture, Johann Dzierzon, appeared.

During his reign, Napoleon strongly supported bee-keeping in France. In his palace in Rambouillet every room, even the bathrooms, were decorated with symbols of bees.

Bee-keeping in Hungary

According to Herodotus, honey was taken from bees on the banks of the Ister (Danube) by the Thracians as long as 2500 years ago. They may have learned to collect honey from the Greeks; that is, they did not make any attempt to domesticate bees but obtained the rare delicacy by robbing the wild bees living in hollow trees or in the crevices of rocks of their reserves.

Bee-keeping in the Danube valley is mentioned several times in ancient scripts. As Strabo tells us, it was Ceneus, a magician from Egypt, adviser to Boerbistas, Prince of the Eastern Goths, who taught bee-farming to the people inhabiting the fields along the Danube.

Priscus *rhetor*, notary to the legate Maximus, visited the court of Attila, king of the Huns by the order of Theodosius II of the Eastern Empire. In his account of his visit he described that members of the delegation were offered mead to drink *(pro vino medam)*. In his books about cultivated plants, Victor Hehn mentions that in the first millennia B.C. linden forests yielding abundant honey, stretched from the Carpathians to the lower reaches of the Danube. This again increases the likelihood that the people living there as early as the seventh–eighth century—Celts, Dacians, Gepids, Sarmatians, Avars, Longobards and Slavs—were engaged in bee-rearing before the arrival of the Hungarians.

According to the inscription on the sarcophagi exhibited in Aquincum Museum, Budapest, legions of Gallic origin took honey-cake moulds made of baked clay with them. In the sixth century the East Roman Emperor, Justinianus, sent an archbishop to the territory of present-day Hungary to further the spread of Christianity. The demand for wax taken from wild bees had greatly increased due to religious ceremonies performed by candle light. (Salamon F.: "Gyertyás szertartások" [Candle Ceremonies]. *Századok, 1881, pp. 643–76.*)

As related by the Catholic bishop Arnold Ipolyi (1823–86), in his *Magyar Mithologia* (Hungarian Mythology), Hungarian tribes were familiar with honey before the conquest of the Carpathian Basin, they even made mead.

The first written document following the conquest of, and settlement in Hungary, dates from the age of Stephen I (1000–38). Dated 1015, it replaces the lost deed of foundation of Pécsvárad monastery dated in 1001, on the occasion of the consecration of the church (*Codex Diplomaticus Hungariae*. 1st vol. pp. 296–302).

The document includes a list of the estates, forests and fields, ploughmen, horses and cattle, drivers, vine-dressers, and several other kinds of craftsmen provided for the monastery. Among them were twelve apiarists *(apiarius)*, who were probably engaged in collecting honey and wax from wild bees living in the forests, since no mention is made of either hives or any apiary in the very detailed list.

Six wax chandlers *(cereariis)* were supposed to press the rest of the honey from the combs and, after cleaning the wax, to sun-bleach it. Candles were then made from the wax in votive symbols of natural colour or painted red. These moulded figures represented feet, eyes and other diseased parts of the body, or symbolized love and fertility. The figures were then sold to pilgrims who sought to remedy their illnesses or praying, expressed their thanks in this way. This custom has survived in Europe to the present day. The wax figurines were cast in baked clay moulds just like in Roman times. It was only much later that moulds carved from pear-wood were generally accepted for making wax, honeycake and marzipan figurines.

The deed of foundation also mentions coopers who made wine-butts, beer kegs and casks for honey.

The five *pistardii,* probably honeycake-makers, made life in the monastery less monotonous with their sweets, and their duties may have included serving virgin combs* with white honey when some celebrity sat at the table.

In the deed of foundation of Zalavár cloister, dated 1019, besides listing the properties, implements and serfs provided, it is stated that "...besides the cultivation of fields and vineyards, and fishing, nobody should disturb them in their bee-keeping..." (Wenczel, Gusztáv: *Árpád-kori új okmánytár* [A New Collection of Documents from the Age of the Árpáds], 1966, vol. 4, pp. 24–27.)

The semi-nomadic ancestors of the Hungarians may well have collected honey in the same way as the ones described by the Russian natural scientist V. K. Arsenev, in his hunters' stories from the Ussuri valley. (Halifman, J. A.: *A méhek* [The Bees], Budapest, 1955.) "...in the summer of 1906 we were having tea in a gamekeeper's house when a little bee appeared on one of the cups on which a drop of honey had been left. After a short while more arrived, sating themselves and then loaded with the sweet liquid, flew away. Murshin the Cossack offered to find out where the bees' nest was. He took the tea cup with the drop of honey in one hand, established the direction of the bees' flight and started off in that direction. After a minute a bee appeared to feed. He followed in the direction it had flown until he lost sight of it. Then he waited until another bee came, loaded itself with honey and left. He followed this one too. So he continued with the next bee and the following ones. Honey-hunting in this way, of course, requires enormous patience. Murshin also undertook to pilfer the combs from the big crevice of a rock. He made a fire and threw smoking branches one after the other into the crevice. When the bees were dazed he climbed up the rocks and cut off the end of one of the combs which was hanging there. In this way he got the finest virgin wax construction filled with honey. He put it into a well-sealed vessel and returned to the hunters. He had to be most careful though, not to let any of the honey leak out, because had the bees recovered from their dazed condition and found the thief of their honey, they could have stung him to death."

The Székelys of Transylvania also had their ancient methods of honey-hunting. They regularly searched for bees' nests and once they had found them, they marked them, and periodically took the honeycombs. The method of finding the nests in the Székely area was to smear a large round wooden plate with honey and fasten it to a pole. Bees gathered, attracted by the fragrance of the honey, imbibed as much as they could. It was then easy to observe their route when they returned to their nest.

In the deed of foundation of Tihany Abbey issued by Andrew I (1047–61) in 1055, we can find references to the domestication of bees. Namely, among the items and people provided there were two apiarists and fifty hives ("vasa"). (*Codex Diplomaticus... ibid.* vol. 1, pp. 388–94).

It is indicative of the development of bee-keeping that honey and mead were soon taxed. King Salomon (1063–74), in 1067 ordered that the inhabitants of Suruk Manor deliver a bucketful of honey per house to the Abbey *(unam idram mellis)* and the people of Dusnok, three cubuluses of mead *(medonem)* (Wenczel, G.: *ibid.* 1966. IV. pp. 24–27).

In his 1075 deed of foundation of Garamszentbenedek Abbey King Géza I (1074–77) do-

* A virgin comb is a comb recently constructed and containing no brood.

nated some apiaries at Balatonszőlős. The inhabitants had to offer up 12 *akós* (1 *akó* is about 12 gallons) of honey.

In 1138 King Béla II, the Blind (1131–41), confirmed the privileges accorded by his father Prince Álmos to the Dömös Provostship, according to which 59 villages had to pay 175 cubuluses of mead.

According to a several hundred years' old description mead was made in Hungary as follows: the honey, diluted with water, was boiled, skimmed and flavoured with spices. For this purpose mostly hops, coriander and basil were used. The liquid was then cooled, poured, into barrels, fermented by adding yeast and then after two or three months' rest, drawn into another barrel. The older the barrel the better it enhanced the aroma of the honey.

The Hungarian kings of the House of Árpád supported the Church—which in turn took sides with them—primarily to consolidate their power, but the Church also played an important role in the field of education and teaching the best contemporary methods of agriculture, including apiculture. This is why prime apiaries were in the possession of monasteries and other religious institutions for centuries.

Honey was very valuable, therefore the first king of Hungary permitted the Church to collect tithes of honey and wax. The kings made every effort to ensure the same income for the treasury, too. In 1278, Ladislas IV, the Cumanian (1262–90) ordered that tax should be levied on each barrel of honey. In later centuries beekeeping serfs were also often compelled to pay a ninth of the fruits of their labour to the landlord.

It was no problem to sell honey even at high prices, as honeycake-makers, physicians, chemists, sorcerers and all kinds of quacks bought much honey, and the makers of candles and votive symbols sought increasing quantities of beeswax. According to data found in archives, not only tax but customs duties and fines could also be paid in honey and wax. Surviving accounts of feasts given by aristocrats show that huge amounts of money were spent on honey on such occasions.

Another sign of fairly advanced apiculture in the twelfth—thirteenth centuries in Hungary was that non-royal benefactors also donated bees, like lord Lieutenant Péter, who granted 10 colonies to the Zászty monastery. (Wenczel, G.: *ibid.* vol. [Borsod County] 1, p. 24.) The wife of Lord Lieutenant Márton, Magdaléna, donated 10 colonies of bees to St. Peter's monastery which, together with a manor called Mura was founded by her husband in Csatár (*Codex Diplomaticus... ibid.* vol. II. p. 92.).

In 1231 Lord Lieutenant Gug offered the wax and honey produced by his bees to meet the requirements of St. Nicholas's chapel built in Dym, so that on great religious feast candles and mead could be distributed among the poor (*Codex Diplomaticus... ibid.* vol. 7, pp. 226–28).

It was noted by György Fejér, that the envoy sent by the King of France to the Tartar Khan in 1150 was offered a honeyed drink, similar to wine. At the time of the Mongol Invasion of Hungary (1241–42) the invaders often robbed hives and made liquor from the honey.

The prelate of Tihany was obliged to give 10 pound of wax annually for the high altar of the church (*Codex Diplomaticus... ibid.* vol. 8, p. 537).

Canon Péter commanded that a candle weighing 10 pounds should be burned at his expense in the Pozsony church on the anniversary of his parents' death.

Master Muthinerius, provost of Szepes, stated in his will of 1273 that half of his bees kept at Luka should be given to the bell-ringer of the Church of St. Martin and the other half to the sexton of the Chapel of the Blessed Virgin Mary

(Knauz, N.: *Monumenta ecclesiae Strigonensis*, vol. 2, pp. 27–28).

Bishop János of Nyitra complained to Archbishop László of Kalocsa who was examining the affairs of the diocese in 1318, that the serfs of Máté Trencsényi (Csák) did not pay an ecclesiastical tithe on bees because the landowner who had stoop up to, and even waged war against the king, kept even that for himself (*Codex Diplomaticus... ibid.* vol. 7, p. 173).

The honey and wax trade of the Transylvanians was so important that the Saxon merchants of Nagyszeben (today Sibiu, Rumania) were, in 1370, given the privilege of being exempted from paying duty by King Louis the Great. At first it only concerned the Székesfehérvár Fair, but later its validity was extended, out of national interest, to Vienna, Bohemia, Dalmatia and Venice. In even later times their consignments went as far as Flanders (*Codex Diplomaticus... ibid.* vol. 9, pp. 297–301).

Bees were also used for defending fortresses in Hungary. Two instances noted are the siege of Németújvár (today Güssing, Austria) in 1289, when the defenders of the stronghold repelled the attacks of Albert I, Prince of Austria, using bees (Engel, J. Ch.: *Geschichte des Ungarischen Reichs*, Vienna, 1813–14), and the siege of Nándorfehérvár (today Belgrade, Yugoslavia) by the Turks, against whom the Hungarians defended the fortified castle by throwing hives and pouring hot tar on them.

There is a vast amount of material in the archives concerning apiculture in medieval Hungary from which the above have been selected as being of particular interest.

In the sixteenth century the greater part of the country was occupied by the Turks. During one and a half centuries of Turkish occupation the inhabitants of these areas adopted several customs from their invaders, like attending public baths, drinking black coffee and, last but not least, the cult of honey so characteristic of oriental peoples. They came to like honeyed drinks, what before then were considered unusually sweet delicacies. In Turkish times honey was so valuable that in many places even indemnity had to be paid in honey. In 1586 the Pasha of Buda demanded a tribute of one thousand *akós* (1 *akó* = about 12 gallons) of honey from the town of Nagykőrös, and two thousand *akó*s from Kecskemét. In the sixteenth century a Christian prisoner fetched one Hungarian pint (*c.* 1.5 litres) of honey in the Buda market-place.

According to a judgement issued by a Kassa (today Košice, Czechoslovakia) Court in 1620, a bee-keeper who had damaged his neighbour's apiary was sentenced to four months' jail besides paying damages. There were much more severe judgements, too. Records were found in the municipal annals of Bártfa (today Bardejov, Czechoslovakia) according to which a suburban woman, Anna Mutter, had been sentenced to be burnt at the stake for robbing bees of their honey. The sentence was carried out in the main square of the town.

According to other records, Daniel Weber, an Austrian commissary, imposed a tribute of 200 *akó*s of honey on the inhabitants of Nagykőrös in 1668.

And now some eloquent data to show how highly honey was valued in those days. It was customary from as early as the sixteenth century that during some important event, like a session of the Diet, the prices of basic commodities were fixed by decree. So it happened on the occasion of the Diet in Pozsony (today Bratislava, Czechoslovakia) in 1563. One pint of honey cost 5 denarii whereas the price of a pound of beef was 2 denarii and a butt (*c.* 25 gallons) of wheat flour fetched 20 denarii. A cartload of shingles sold at 25 denarii. A pint of honey cost 18 denarii on the Braşov market whereas a pint of fat cost 8 denarii.

Migratory bee-keeping was known in mountainous areas in the seventeenth century. The hives were carried on carts and by mules to the flowering meadows at higher altitudes and to honey-yielding pinewoods.

Just as the forests surrounding Nuremberg were called Bienengarten (bee-garden) on account of the numbers of nectar plants and trees flourishing there, similarly, there was an open woodland in Beszterce-Naszód County mentioned by the same name where, according to tradition, there had been large apiaries.

Several surnames and place-names testify to the fact that bees were kept all over the country: Méhes (*méh* = bee), Méhi, Méhész, Méhkerék, Méhtelek, Mézes (*méz* = honey), Kaptár (= hive), Rajka (*raj* = swarm). One of the fields in Nagybelic (Nyitra County) was called Celne (*vcelne* = bee in Slovak).

The Church often punished scandalous behaviour, such as cursing or fornication by the delivery of wax as penance. Guilds demanded apprentices' fees in wax and penalties for not attending the funeral of a master of the guild were also payable in beeswax. Alternatively, the latter could be paid in mead which was then drunk at the burial feast.

Counties and the lords of the fortified castles demanded contributions towards war expenses in wax, whose value did not change, and part of the soldiers' pay was given in mead (*Szondy György Album*, edited and published by Lajos Pongrácz, Esztergom–Ipolyság, 1885).

The first book of apiculture entitled *Tractatus de apibus,* was written by Miklós Horhi, the head of the Rákóczi family's Nagyvárad apiary. For his outstanding services he was given the title "Master Apiarist". In 1707 Prince Ferenc Rákóczi II made the honey trade a state monopoly on territories controlled by him, so that the income from this source would contribute to the costs of his War of Independence (1703–11). In 1707 he demanded 109 *icce*s (1 *icce* = about ⅕ of a gallon) of honey from the town of Kassa for his kitchen. (*Magyar Gazdaságtörténeti Szemle,* 1895, p. 185.)

According to superstition a swarm of bees flying into a courtyard brought misfortune. One of the generals of Ferenc Rákóczi II, Miklós Ber-

ÚJ TALÁLMÁNY

és

IGEN JELES MÓD,

Mellyet

A' MÉH-KASOKNAK,

és

KÓPÚKNEK FORMÁJÁRÚL

'S AZOKNAK NÉPESITÉSÉRŐL.

A' Méhes Gazdáknak, a' ſok Kóltségtűl, és fáradságtúl (mellyet az ereſztés alkalmatoſságával kéntelenek tenni) meg-mentésérűl, és a' ſzegény Méheknek-is, gonoſz meg-jutalmaztatáſok alól, mellyel tulajdon kereſ-ményekért ſzoktak nékik a' Gazdák fizetni fel-ſzabaditásokrúl, 's több eddig rendeletlenűl gyakorlott-dolgoknak-is rendeſſebb módgyairúl.

HÉT ESZTENDEI PRÓBÁI-UTÁN IRT

EZEKNEK TALALÓJA

GEDDE JÁNOS,

és A' GRESHAIMBÉLI

KIRÁLYI TÁRSASÁG-IS

Helyben hagyott.

Nyomtattatott Londonban M. DC. LXXVI. Eſztendőben És Iſmét ugyan ott meg-Újjittatott M DCC. XXII. Ángliai Nyelvbűl Némnetre Fordittatott M. DCC. XXVII. És Újjobban Ki-bocsáttatott M. DCC. XXIX. Eſztendőben.

János (John) Gedde: *A' méh-kasoknak és köpüknek formájárúl* (Forms of Skeps and Bee-hives...) Printed in London, in 1676

csényi, reported to the Prince that bees had landed on one of his guns at Érsekújvár (today Nové Zámky, Czechoslovakia). Whatever the reason, it is a fact that the Battle of Érsekújvár was lost in 1710.

At the beginning of the eighteenth century bee-keeping lost ground for a while. Sugar, appearing on the market in increasing quantities, made honey less of a valuable commodity, and the demand for wax also slackened in the wake of spreading Protestantism; fewer candles were burned in puritanical Protestant churches.

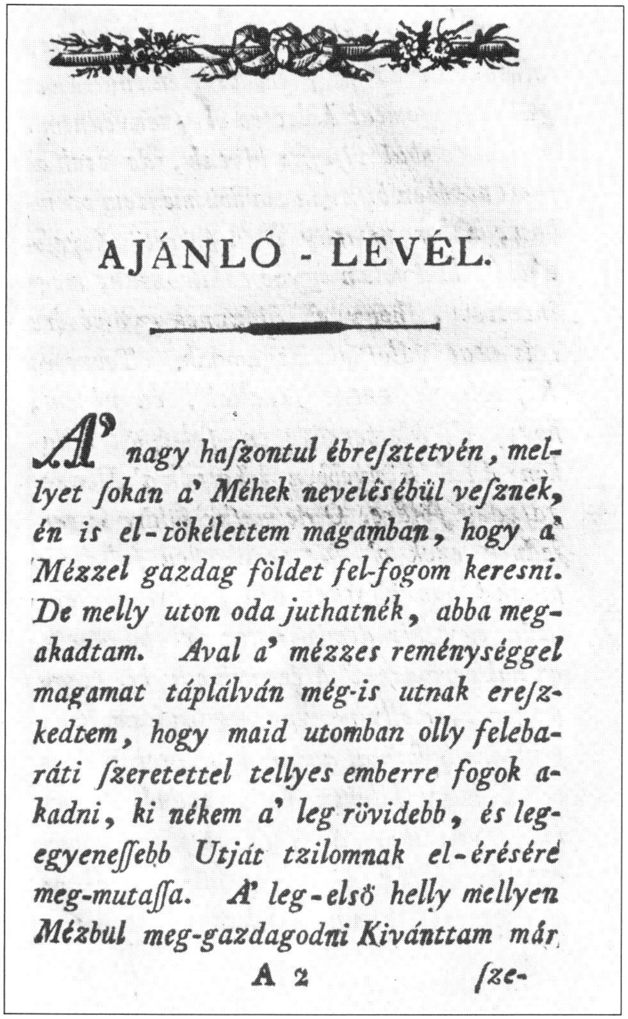
AJÁNLÓ - LEVÉL.

A' nagy haſzontul ébreſztetvén, mellyet ſokan a' Méhek nevelésébül veſznek, én is el-tökéllettem magamban, hogy a' Mézzel gazdag földet fel-fogom keresni. De melly uton oda juthatnék, abba megakadtam. Aval a' mézzes reménységgel magamat táplálván még-is utnak ereſzkedtem, hogy maid utomban olly felebaráti ſzeretettel tellyes emberre fogok akadni, ki nékem a' leg rövidebb, és legegyeneſſebb Utját tzilomnak el-érésére meg-mutaſſa. A' leg-elsö helly mellyen Mézbul meg-gazdagodni Kivánttam már

A 2 *ſze-*

János Bogsch: *Természetes méhek neveléseiről való rövid oktatás* (Short Handbook on Breeding Natural Bees) 1795. Ajánlás (Dedication)

In her rescript of November 8th, 1765, Maria Theresa (1740–80) drew the attention of the Hungarian and Transylvanian governments to apiculture. It was in the same year that the first bee-keepers' association was formed in the Banat. In 1768 the council of the governor-general sent a circular to all counties stressing the importance of supporting bee-farming.

In 1770 an academy of apiculture was founded in Vienna to which Hungarian bee-keepers were invited and were offered free board and lodging. It was indicative of the interest shown that four people wanted to attend from Sopron county alone. They were the ones about whom the council of the governor general asked for a report stating the marks they had been given and describing how they had made use of the acquired knowledge. In 1775 a royal letter patent again invited attendance at the academy. One of the 16 points of the open letter patent placed particular emphasis on the fact that the instruction was gratis.

In Austria and Moravia Maria Theresa abolished tithes on apicultural products. Bee-keepers were to pay not more than 2 *krajcárs* (*c.* 2 pence) to the land owner for the area occupied by their hives. Any hindrance to bee-farming, including the trade in apicultural products, was forbidden.

Bee-masters were entitled to look for their swarms within 24 hours even in foreign territories, and to remove them after a reasonable refund of costs. It was forbidden to kill bees. Those doing so had to pay double the sum of damages.

The queen appointed József Toldy, supposedly a graduate of the Vienna Academy of

Apiculture, inspector of apiculture for the territory of Hungary. She ordered that in the military boarding schools at Vác and Szenc (today Senec, Czechoslovakia) apiculture should be taught alongside military sciences.

In 1741 apicultural exports amounted to 65 thousand forints. By the end of Maria Theresa's reign they had risen to 300 tons of wax and 400 tons of honey valuing more than 350 thousand forints.

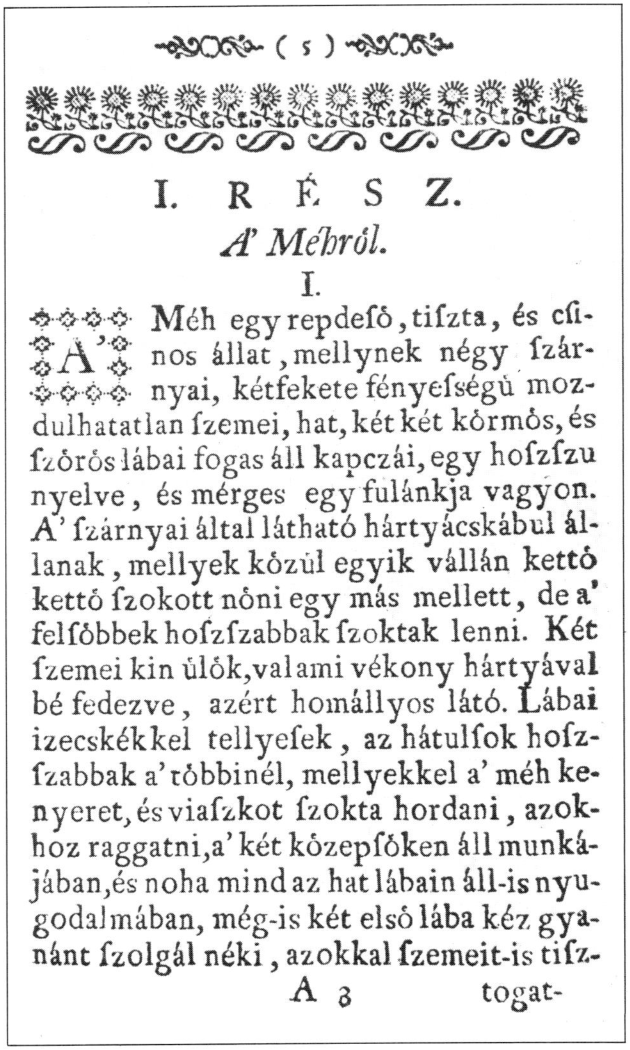

(5)

I. R É S Z.

A' Méhről.

I.

A' Méh egy repdeſő, tiſzta, és cſinos állat, mellynek négy ſzárnyai, kétfekete fényeſségű mozdulhatatlan ſzemei, hat, két két kőrmős, és ſzőrős lábai fogas áll kapczái, egy hoſzſzu nyelve, és mérges egy fulánkja vagyon. A' ſzárnyai által látható hártyácskábul állanak, mellyek közül egyik vállán kettő kettő ſzokott nőni egy más mellett, de a' felſőbbek hoſzſzabbak ſzoktak lenni. Két ſzemei kin ülők, valami vékony hártyával bé fedezve, azért homállyos látó. Lábai izecskékkel tellyeſek, az hátulſok hoſzſzabbak a' többinél, mellyekkel a' méh kenyeret, és viaſzkot ſzokta hordani, azokhoz raggatni, a' két közepſőken áll munkájában, és noha mind az hat lábain áll-is nyugodalmában, még-is két elſő lába kéz gyanánt ſzolgál néki, azokkal ſzemeit-is tiſz-

A 3 togat-

Lőrincz Pálffy: *Erdélyi méhecske* (The Small Transylvanian Bee). Kolozsvár, 1762. Title-page: I. rész. A Méhről (Part I. Of Bees)

Joseph II (1780–90) closed the Academy of Apiculture in Vienna in 1781, but in 1783 ordered that cottagers should be taught the trade; he appointed teachers of apiculture whose duties included demonstrative and practical education. He also ordered that good honey-yielding linden and acacia trees should be planted along roadsides. Despite all this, apiculture fell back in a few years to the pre-1741 level.

In 1797 Count György Festetics founded the agricultural academy *Georgikon,* where apiculture was one of the subjects. The first lecturer on apiculture was Ferenc Pete who published his work under the pseudonym "Nemzeti Gazda" (national farmer). He makes mention of the *köpü,* a primitive form of hive, which differed from the skep inasmuch as it was not round and "was made of boards".

Apiculture was also taught at the agricultural and industrial school founded by Kristóf Nákó in Nagyszentmiklós in Torontál County (today Sînnicolau Mare, Rumania).

Forty-two books appeared in Hungary about bee-keeping between 1759 and 1817 in Hungarian, Latin and German.

Ehrenfels, a bee-farmer who owned one thousand hives, was a lecturer on apiculture at the Vienna Academy of Apiculture which had reopened. In 1816 he elaborated a proposal according to which a bee-keeping society should be formed to set up 30 apiaries of 150 hives each on a territory of about 3–4 square miles. In the ninth year it would result (as he explained in detail) in a divisible profit of seventy-five thousand florins. Bee-keeping was conducted with increasing awareness of scientific and economic considerations.

In the middle of the nineteenth century the movable-framed hives of the German Johann

Dzierzon and the American Lorenzo Lorraine Langstroth, revolutionized the world's apiculture. There were promising experiments in Hungary too, but development was impeded by the economic recession following in the wake of the defeat of the War of Independence in 1848–49.

ÁNGLIAI

MÉHES KERT

MELY

A' Méhekkel való bánáſnak meſterségét, és titkait ſzemünk elejbe terjeſzti. Azokat, mellyeket a' régi, és új Irók e' dologrúl írtak, meg-jobítva, rövid ſummába foglallja,

ÉS

A' Méh-kaſok el-kéſzitésének egy új, és igen haſznos módjával együtt, a' Méhes-Gazdáknak eddig fel-talált minden módoknál haſznoſſabb, keveſebb költségü, és fáradságú rendet nyújt,

MELLYET

Ki-adott Ángliai nyelven

GEDDE JÁNOS.

és helyben hagyott a' *London*-béli Királyi Tudós Tárſaság 1721-dik Eſztendőben

MOST PEDIG

Német nyelvből Tekéntetes Nemes

SZATTMÁRY KIRÁLY GYÖRGY

T. N. Borſod Vármegye Törvény-ſzékének egyik Tagja, a' Méhes-Gazdáknak haſznokra Magyar nyelvre forditott, 's-maga különös jegyzésével-is meg-nagyobbitott. Máſodſzor ki-nyomtattatott.

EGERBEN,

Nyomt. a' Püspöki Oskola betőivel 1768

János (John) Gedde: *Angliai méhes kert* (Bee Gardens in England). Printed in Eger with the printing press of the episcopal school, in 1768. From Ferenc Széchényi's library. Title-page

The *Bienenzeitung,* in which the new ideas of J. Dzierzon were published, had several Hungarian subscribers and correspondents, doctors, landowners and clergymen. According to contemporary data the Nyitra-Zsámbokrét district in Nyitra County offered especially good conditions for bee-keeping.

The first society for apiculture in Hungary was formed in Székesfehérvár in 1841. In 1844 another society was founded in the Barcaság, but none of them survived long.

In 1848–49 and 1873 no bee-keepers' association was established. In 1873 in Buziás (Temes County) the *Délmagyarországi Méhészeti Egyesület* (Apicultural Society of Southern Hungary) was set up for bee-masters in the Banat and in Arad county. A year later they launched a trade journal entitled *Ungarische Biene* edited by the Gand brothers. It was only in 1879 that the *Országos Magyar Méhészeti Egyesület* (National Hungarian Apicultural Association) was formed, which then took over the trade paper which had switched over to the Hungarian language, and had the title *Magyar Méh* (Hungarian Bees). In 1880 the *Erdélyrészi Méhészeti Egyesület* (Apicultural Association of Transylvanian Regions) began its operations in Kolozsvár (today Cluj, Rumania).

In 1892 the National Association and the Society of Southern Hungary merged, and no further structural changes took place until 1945. The present organizational structure of apiculture in Hungary will be dealt with in another chapter.

The Honeybee

"...for so work the honey-bees,
Creatures that by a rule nature teach
The act of order to a peopled kingdom.
They have a king and officers of sorts;
Where some, like magistrates, correct at home,
Others, like merchants, venture trade abroad,
Others, like soldiers, armed in their stings,
Make boot upon the summer's velvet buds;
Which pillage they with merry march bring home
To the tent-royal of their emperor:
Who, busied in his majesty, surveys
The singing masons building roofs of gold,
The civil citizens kneading up the honey,
The poor mechanic porters crowding in
Their heavy burdens at his narrow gate,
The sad-ey'd justice, with his surly hum,
Delivering o'er to executors pale
The lazy yawning drone."

(Shakespeare: King Henry V. Act I)

The ancients thought of honey as a gift of heavenly powers. They believed that the dew bees collected from the flowers to make honey from had fallen from the stars. This belief was only discounted in the palmy days of the Roman Empire.

In his play written at the end of the sixteenth century, Shakespeare pictured the life of bees modelled on human society. He thought of the social structure of his day as the only possible one, so why should bees not live in the same way with a king, officials, servants, merchants, and good-for-nothing drones delivered into the hands of the executioner.

Great changes occurred in the world during the following one hundred years, but the comparison drawn between human societies and that of bees was to endure for a long time.

In 1794, a book appeared in Hungary written by György Handerla, a specialist in apiaries, entitled "Új méhész vagyis a' méheknek magyar hazánkhoz alkalmazott gondviselése, melly rövid kérdésekbe és feleletekbe foglalt tanítással megmutatja mint kell Télen, Nyáron a' méhekkel bánni" (The new bee-keeper's method of providing for bees, adapted to Hungary, which gives instruction in the form of short questions and answers on how bees should be treated in winter and summer). Handerla described his observations as follows:

"... perceivable attributes are as follows: first that bees exemplify a Monarchy, that is a Ruling Principality... And all this can be seen not in a glass vessel but in a skep turned upside down, with the help of a magnifying glass, although not clearly."

He also describes the interpretation adopted by those who had travelled abroad.

"... only one queen, who is the leader of the whole swarm of bees, and is also called the mother bee, pours and lays the eggs one by one into the little chambers of cells and combs..."

The author, however, did not accept the suggestion that the queen would not produce so many superfluous drones if, indeed, she alone laid all the eggs into the cells.

The book's poetic language makes exciting reading with many surprisingly logical conclusions.

Research workers and practising bee-keepers have observed the conditions governing honey production to this day, and new, surprising disclosures are published almost daily.

The "leading lady" of honey production, the honeybee (*Apis mellifica L.*) belongs to the order of hymenoptera.

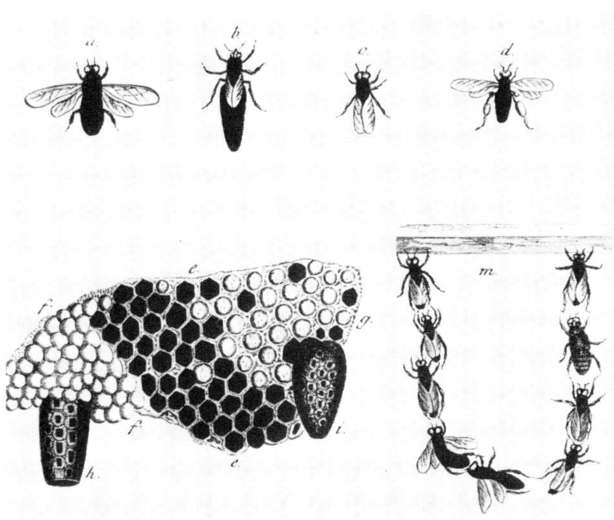

Drawing from Friedrich Bertuchi's work entitled *Bilderbuch zum Nutzen und Vergnügen der Jugend.*
(a) male bee or drone;
(b) "queen bee of which there is only one in the whole skep";
(c) forager bee; there are about 30,000 of them in the skep "they do all the work";
(d) forager flying;
(e) a piece of comb;
(m) "a chain of bees".

The most frequently bred varieties of the bee native to Central Europe are the Italian bee (*Apis mellifica varietas liqustica*) and the Caucasian bee (*Apis mellifica remipacaes*). It was these varieties which replaced the native bees of smaller stature in North America, which stored very little honey in their barely accessible nests. The "bugs"—that is what individual bees are called in certain places—are usually light in colour in the first days of life. Italian bees are yellow whilst Caucasian bees and bees of the Banat are almost black and very hairy all over.

More distant relatives of the bee family are wasps, bumble bees and ants whose appearance is somewhat similar to that of bees, but their way of life and behaviour are utterly different.

Bees make honey from the nectar of flowers and the sweet secretions of other parts of plants. They suck up the sugary solution and transform it with the help of the enzymes in their honey sacs. They mix it with their own proteins and hormones and, finally, store it in the cells of their combs, where they condense and ripen it. All these instinctive and conditioned activities serve the purpose of building up reserves for themselves and for their progeny in times of scarcity of food.

In order to collect the sweet juices, which also contain several other substances, bees have special organs in their heads: their complicated mouthparts include a labellum ("spoon" of tongue), the proboscis, and the glossa which moves back and forth, like a piston within the tube of the proboscis. On the bee's head there are thousands of olfactory nerves, sensory organs, special visual fasciculi and also eyes. The weight of their brains is 1/170 of the weight of their bodies, an indication of a highly developed nervous system within the insect kingdom. The corresponding proportion for may-flies, for instance is 1 to 3500.

The pharyngeal gland or brood-food gland is the organ for making larval food (royal jelly) and it also directs the feeding of the progeny. It is part of a bee's head as is the masticatory wax gland which protrudes from its mouth.

The six legs and the four membraneous wings which serve for walking, flying, transportation and moving, are on the thorax behind the bee's head. According to J. A. Halifman, a Soviet researcher on bees, their wings are able to carry them at a speed of 20 to 60 kilometres an hour. They also cause such a current within the hive that 10 per cent of the weight of the thin liquid honey deposited in the cells evaporates within 24 hours. Their legs are adapted to raise the body in any direction, so a bee can take off from any position.

In the bend at the joint of the third and fourth segments of the first pair of legs, there is a cavity which is used for the cleaning of the palps or antennae, and there is another on the upper segment of the hind pair of legs, which is called the corbicula or pollen basket. This is where bees carry pollen from the flower to the hive. The working bee, which is covered with tiny hairs all over its body, collects the pollen which sticks to

Bee hives Illustration of the Hungarian edition of *Bee Gardens in England* by János (John) Gedde. Eger, 1768

its belly, or its head or has fallen on its back, with the comb and brush on its hind legs. Then through the groove of the leg, it slips the pollen into the basket, and then, using all its legs while hovering over the flower, presses it into a neat little grain. In this way, subject to the consistency of the pollen, a bee can collect about 8–18 mg at one time.

The third part of a bee's body is the abdomen, which, viewed from outside, consists of five annuli. Within this is the honey sac into which a bee can suck up about 20 mg nectar at one time. The transformation of the nectar into a thin honey solution—as mentioned—begins as soon as it reaches the honey sac, first of all through the action of the invertase enzyme.

On reaching home the bee empties the contents of its honey sac into the cells of the comb for condensation, or into the mouths of the young nurse-bees who busy themselves in the hive.

The digestive organs performing the bodily functions of the bee itself are also within the abdomen. They supply the necessary energy for maintaining body heat and moving about. In order to carry nectar into the hive from a distance of one kilometre, the bee needs the energy gained from 1.5 mg of honey, distributed to the various organs by the blood. The abdomen contains the heart, the lungs and the kidneys as well as the female weapon, the sting, which is used primarily for defence but also for killing the drones which become superfluous by the end of the summer. The scent gland, which is probably to help the other bees find their way to honey-yielding flowers, available pollen and sweet fluids, is at the end of the upper side of the abdomen. It is also possible that this gland is the source of the characteristic honey and wax scent common to all honey and wax, and which is also produced artificially under the names honey flavour and wax flavour.

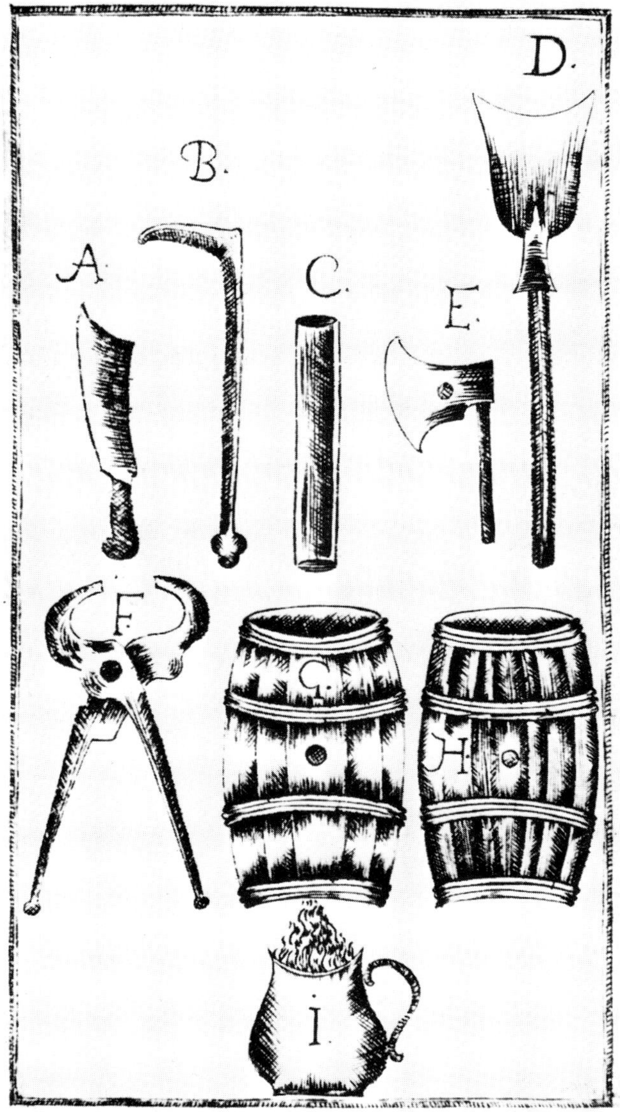

Bee-keeping tools. Illustration from the Hungarian edition of *Bee Gardens in England* by János (John) Gedde. Eger, 1768

The organ which produces beeswax and secretes it in the form of a plate is under the annules on the lower side of the abdomen. Beeswax is the most important building material of the bees. The hexagonal cells of the comb are also made of it. Bees store ripe honey in the cells of the comb covered with little plates of wax. Pollen, collected for feeding the brood, is also kept in such cells, mixed with a little nectar or water and honey and rammed down by the heads of the workers.

It is also in these cells where the offspring of the bees are brought up. Bees, just like other insects, only grow in the larval stage; they then become chrysalises, transform and emerge from the cells of the comb in a fully developed state.

The hexagonal cells of the comb can be said to be the most perfect creations of Nature; they make the best use of the available space, their vertical walls are at a distance of 5 mm from each other and the distance of the opposite corners is slightly less than 7 mm. The diameter of a working bee is 4.6 mm, so there is enough room for it to fit in, even if more than one generation of larvae were raised in the cell, leaving several pupa skins behind which strengthen but also thicken the walls of the cell. The hexagonal form also ensures excellent stability enabling the thin, white virgin comb to hold honey, and also endure the centrifugal force by which the honey is extracted from the comb. In constructing hexagonal cells the bees make the most economical use of the wax. Much more beeswax would be needed if, for instance, the cells were round.

The bee colony

The members of a colony are:

—the queen, who continually lays eggs;

—the female workers, with their undeveloped reproductive organs, who fly to the flowers and other plants, collect nectar and pollen and also do jobs within the hive, and

—the drones, ensuring that the young queen is inseminated once and for life.

Life in the hive

Bees store the honey and pollen collected during the summer in the cells of the comb. When the cold weather sets in, the flowers wither away and there is less work. The bees, whose body temperature varies in accordance with the air temperature, gather around the queen to try to ensure a temperature of about 14 °C for her. To produce the necessary thermal energy they have to move and eat. The colder the winter the more is consumed from the reserves. A colony spending the winter in the open needs 4 to 5 kilos, whereas if they are in a closed place where there are no subzero temperatures, half this amount is enough. If a colony is kept at around 8 °C even less honey, or sugar is sufficient.

If the temperature of the swarm drops below 8 °C the existence of the colony is in danger. If a bee remains alone in the open it will be numbed even on a cool summer night, and will only come back to life when warmed up by the sunshine. Bees in a wintering swarm will always try to get into the centre of the cluster, so the ones already warmed up there will be pushed towards the surface. The colder the winter, the smaller the cluster will be so that the surface area in contact with the cold air which loses heat, will be the smallest possible.

When the temperature outside reaches 12 to 14 °C the first bees appear in the narrowed entrance, modified for the winter, and begin first to clean themselves, and then perhaps to carry water into the hive. If on such a day a woman hangs freshly-washed sheets on a clothes-line in the open, she will have the unpleasant surprise of seeing that the bees have stained them with little black spots.

In Hungary when mild days arrive sometimes as early as the end of January or the first days of February, the queen starts her work. She checks the cells already cleaned by the workers, gets into each of them in turn, then comes out backwards and lays an egg into it. The eggs hatch in three to four days and the larva stage follows.

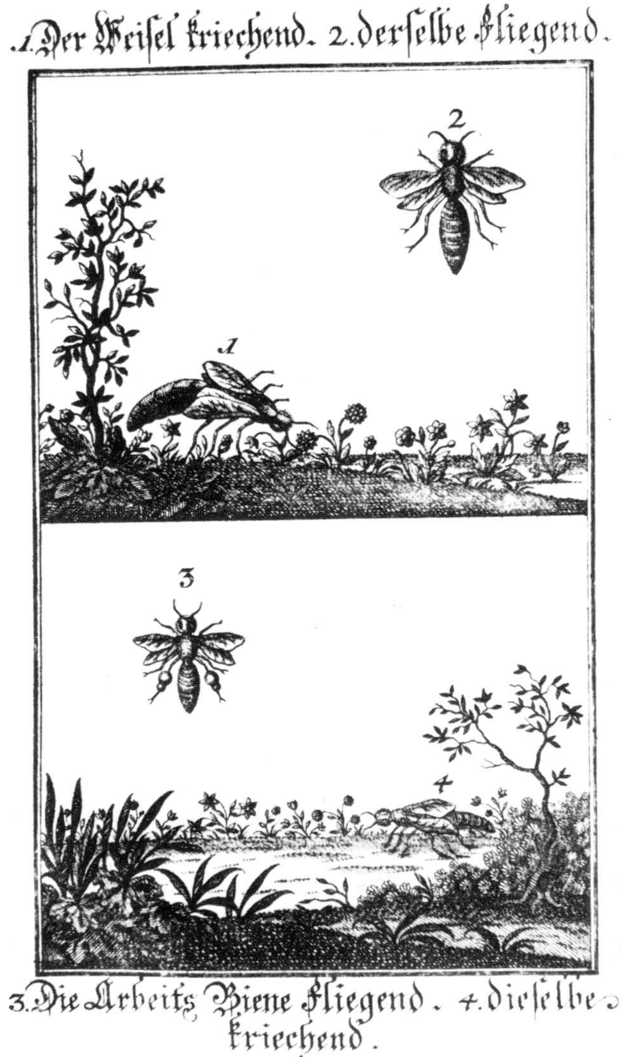

Picture of a queen and of a worker bee from the book entitled *Vezető a méhészkedéshez* (A Guide to Bee-keeping). Pozsony, Leipzig, 1773

The larvae are fed by nurse-bees with royal jelly, honey, and pollen mixed with the secretions of their pharyngeal gland, for about six days. During this period the larvae increase their original weight 1000 to 1500 times. Their diet will subsequently be changed according to the future of the larva, i.e. whether it will be a worker, a drone or a queen. The developed larva prepares a pellicle for itself from its glandular secretions. Then the nurse-bees cover the cells with lids of wax and seal them. The larvae, after emptying the undigested part of their food into the bottom of the cell, are transformed within the pellicle into bees, and emerge from the cell. Worker bees push off the flat wax caps while the drones deal with the curved ones.

A newly emerged young worker bee will clean both itself and the empty cells for two-three days and then feed and nurse the brood, i.e. the individuals developing in the cells (this is why it is called a nurse-bee at this stage) and when the larvae are big enough, it will seal their cells with the wax scales made by itself. In the following twenty days it does other jobs in the hive like using its wings as ventilators at the entrance, changing the air warmed up in the hive. Young worker bees also stand sentry at the entrance lest foreigners should break into the hive, take over the nectar collected by the foragers, condense it using a method similar to gargling in their honey sacs and mouths and then carry it into the new cells. They build new cells of wax scales and cover the ones filled with ripe honey, as Shakespeare puts it, with "roofs of gold". The simile is very apt. Namely the caps are not perpendicular to the cell walls but are at a slight slant with the opening on top so that even liquid nectar will not easily spill out of them.

By the time a bee has done its time of service within the hive its brood-food gland has degenerated, but the life functions of bees generally adapt themselves to the requirements. The workers for example, who emerge from the cell from the end of August to mid-October will only have to perform nursing functions in February, when the queen has started to lay eggs.

When the number of young bees is sufficiently high and the pollen and nectar flow is sufficiently promising, the time for constructing and filling the drone cells with eggs has come. Drones, unlike worker bees are only raised in the spring

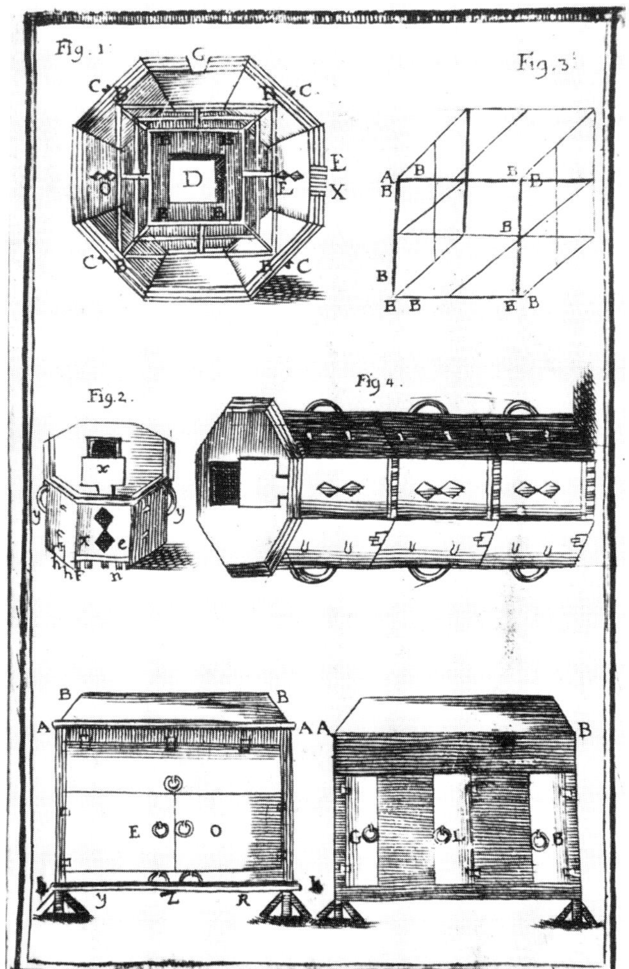

Bee finders and hives. Illustration from the Hungarian edition of *Bee Gardens in England* by János (John) Gedde. Eger, 1768

and early summer. When the egg is not fertilized from the copulatory pouch of the queen it will produce a drone, whereas fertilized eggs will rear workers or queens. If, for some reason the queen dies, drone eggs can be laid by a worker bee substituting for her. It is worth mentioning that although drones are stouter, shorter and sometimes even smaller than worker bees, they need more time to develop fully. The queen, on the other hand, develops quicker than any of them as a result of the special food (royal jelly) she is fed. A larva destined to be a queen will receive this food from the third day until the end. When the pollen and nectar flow is satisfactory the construction of queen cells is started on the combs. In some cases more than one queen is reared at the same time. Normally there cannot be more than one queen in a hive, so an old queen leaves the hive with some of the workers to start a new life. The old queen does not fly too far as her ovary is already full of developing eggs. The bees of such a first swarm will fly to a nearby branch, roof or leaves and form a cluster there. The cluster is then taken by the bee-keeper and put into a skep prepared in advance for this purpose and transferred by shaking or throwing it into the appointed hive. Some bee-keepers put a honeycomb into the hive to ensure the continued existence of the swarm. The bees sate themselves with honey before swarming and set about work in the new dwelling place. They secrete wax and build cells, other collect pollen and nectar, and the queen is busy laying her eggs. Bee-keepers like early swarms because spring-swarming leaves enough time for the colony to develop well by the summer.

In olden times they even made a verse about it. (Brehm: *Tierleben*. Vol. 9, p. 213)

A swarm in May
is worth a freight of hay,
A swarm in June
A good fat hen,
A swarm in July
Not even a feather-broom.

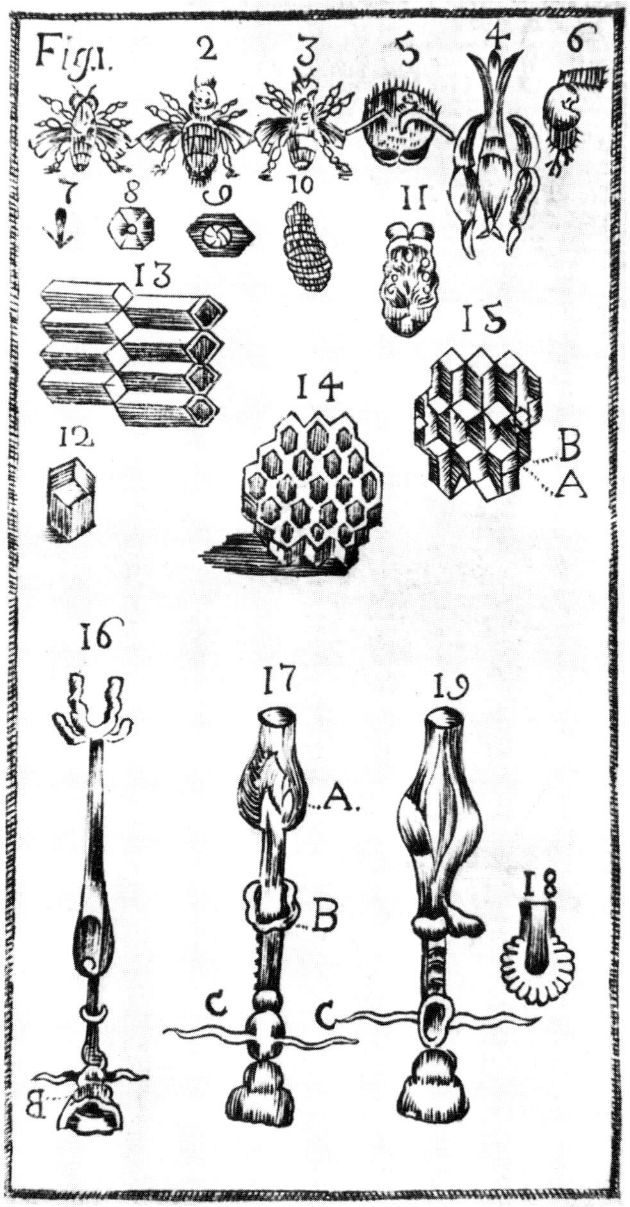

Varieties of bees, kinds of cells. Illustration from the Hungarian edition of *Bee Gardens in England* by János (John) Gedde. Eger, 1768

Apple blossom with bees

The queen bee and the workers cover and protect the larvae

A bee stinging

A queen cell

Workers' pre-dance conference

Expelled drones at the beginning of August

A bee's sting with the drop of poison

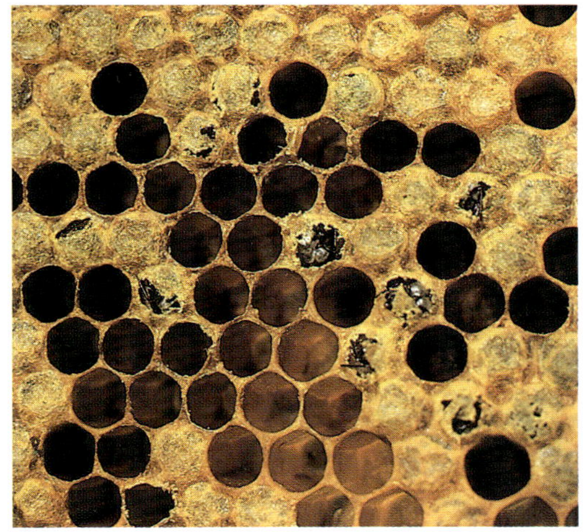

Workers

Bees on a piece of comb

Bees emerging from the covered brood cells

A group of bees

Bees on the comb (detail)

A honey-collecting forager

Apiarist examining the combs in a long hive

Hive entrance with bees

Cross-section of a comb with pupae

Bees swarm on a stake

Egg-laying queen with workers

Anthropomorphous domicile for bees. A female figure with a semicircular entrance. Height: 118 cm. Ethnographical Museum, Budapest

Anthropomorphous domiciles for bees. Cylindrical female figure in a frock which was originally red. The male figure was found in Felsőtóti, Bars County. Ethnographical Museum, Budapest

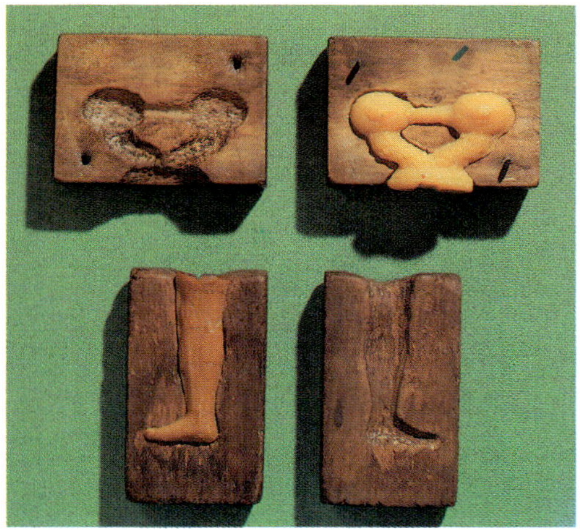

Drone

An apothecary's vessels for honey from the eighteenth–nineteenth centuries. Semmelweis Museum of Medical History, Budapest. (Photographs by Attila Károly)

Votive offerings; wax figures used in folk therapy. Semmelweis Museum of Medical History, Budapest. (Photograph by Attila Károly)

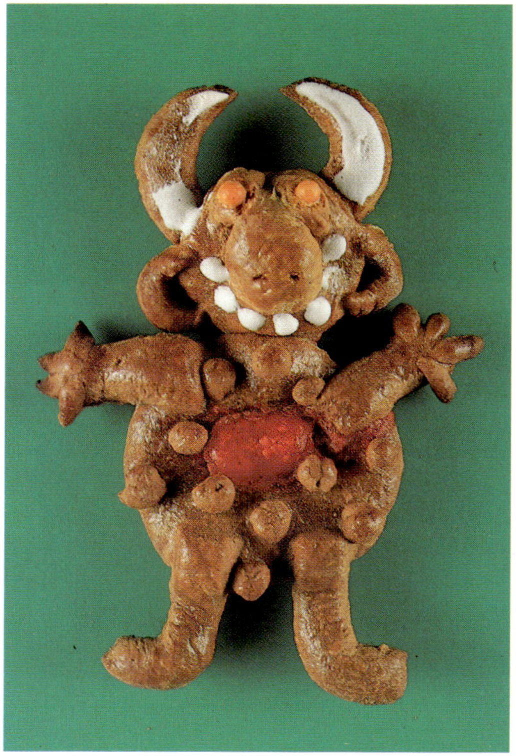

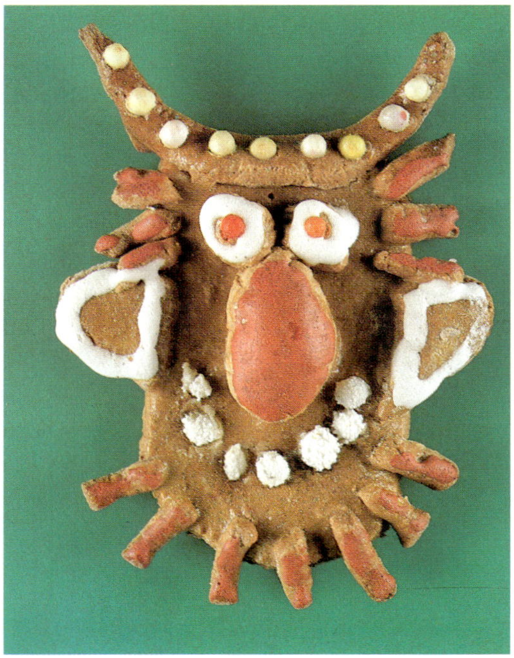

Honeycake mould by Éva Gaál, graphic designer.
Devil's head, cock and mask. (Photographs by Péter Varga)

In the meantime the young queen emerges from her cell, and emitting a characteristically loud call, cleans herself and prepares to be fertilized by one or more drones in a mating flight. When her seminal vesicle is full of semen, she will return to the hive to commence laying eggs. A queen can usually lay 1000 to 1500 eggs within 24 hours but, in exceptional cases, this number may be as large as 3000. Older queens lay fewer eggs so they are replaced every two or three years, although a queen could serve her colony for about seven to eight years.

It sometimes happens that a second queen emerges from her cell and a life-and-death struggle ensues because one of them must die. In his great work *Tierleben* Brehm described such a fight as follows:

"Both queens emerged from their cells at almost the same time. When they caught sight of each other they dashed towards each other in such a fury that their palps got into one another's mouths; head pressed against head, chest against chest and abdomen against abdomen, but they could achieve nothing, neither of them could gain the upper hand. They let go of each other and withdrew. A few moments later the attack resumed with the same result until with a twist, one of them got hold of the other's wing, climbed on her and inflicted a mortal wound upon her."

There is also a division of labour among the bees working outside the skep or hive.

—There are scouts who look for the best, most efficiently exploitable stores of nectar, pollen or honeydew and

—there are foragers who, following the instructions of the scouts, collect and carry the honey found after landing on flowers and plants.

Life in the open; the dance of the bees

In his book about the life of bees, J. A. Halifman describes his observations and those of others as follows:

"The scouts look ceaselessly, not only in the spring but all the year round, for the best bee pastures. Scientific research workers noticed, while observing bees in a glass-walled hive on waxen honeycombs visible from all sides, that some bees were highly sensitive to lamp light while others did not care but went on with their work. The restless bees were lured by the lamp light into a glass corridor which could be opened from above, and was situated between the entrance and the interior of the hive. They were marked with white paint and returned to the hive. The next morning the marked bees were among the first to leave the hive and soon returned with their find. They were received by bees in the hive who took the liquid honey which had been transported in their honey sacks, and transferred it to the cells. When the last drop appeared on the foragers' mouth they licked it off. Then the unburdened bee, who had come home with the treasure, started to dance on an empty part of the comb indicating that it had found an abundant source of pollen or at least one which was worth exploiting. After a few seconds it continued its dance on the other side of the comb walking in circles of 6 to 8 mm diameter. According to research workers this means that it had found a bee pasture close at hand. The dance also expresses the distance and the direction of the nectar. On another occasion the returning scout's dance followed the curves of the number 8 which meant that the nectar or pollen fit for gathering was at a greater distance. So it defined the distance and the direction. The other bees close by imitated the dance."

J. A. Comenius: *Orbis Sensualium Pictus.* 1685. Honey-harvest. "They make little hexagonal cells and fill them with honey liquid, the sweetness of herbs, and they make comb honey".

Dr. Pál Zoltán Örösi, the leading apicultural researcher in Hungary observed in recent decades that distance is indicated by a certain number of flicks of the abdomen during the dance which the bees understand exactly. Those imitating the dance rub themselves against the dancer taking some of the pollen stuck to its hair during collecting and also carry its scent. It is certain that they get even more detailed information which has yet to be deciphered by apicultural researchers.

After receiving instructions, the foragers make a "bee-line" for the flowers. Bees usually follow a straight line from the hive to the pasture, if there is a forest in between they fly over the trees, and return the same way. They only take a more sheltered route among trees when there are strong gusts of wind. As it has been stated that the pollen and nectar always originate from the same species as the samples taken in by the scouts, it is assumed that the bees do not alight anywhere before reaching their goal, nor do they yield to the temptation of other colours, shapes or scents.

Bees collect nectar from the same variety of flowers as long as possible, enabling bee-keepers to extract pure honeys.

Experiments have shown that bees find their way firstly by recognizing shapes then colours. The difference between their sight as compared to that of man, is that they take red for black and mix up green and yellow. The third colour they recognize is blue. They also rely on scent when attempting to reach their destination. With its 6000 olfactory nerves a bee can distinguish 30 to 40 scents.

The worker bee establishes the appropriate flight altitude before it starts collecting. It takes off but then returns for several more take-offs. It is inexperienced as yet, only familiar with flowers from which the other bees collect, so it will also collect nectar from there. It finds its direction instinctively relying on the points given by the hive, the nectar plant and the sun. It will find flowers along the imaginary line which could be drawn from the hive to the sun and also ones which are in the opposite direction.

When bee pastures are rich, a forager can survive the heavy work for two or three weeks only, then it will die. Workers, on the other hand, who shed their pellicles in August or September, will live for six to seven months until the new generation of bees reach the age when they can go out collecting. Then the bee which has survived winter will fail to return to the colony one day; either on its way back, or in front of the entrance it will die a lonely death.

A drone will commence his life during April or May when new swarms need queens and virgin queens need to be fertilized. To ensure fertilization the number of drones is very high, 1000 or 1500 but exceptionally it also may happen

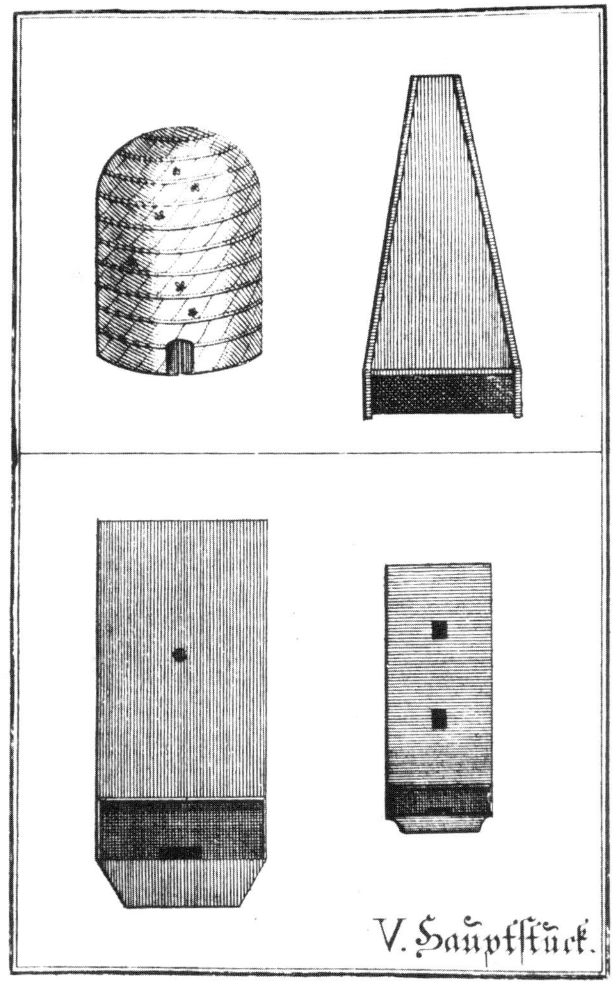

Forms of skeps and other domiciles for bees made of straw and wood. *Vezető a méhészkedéshez* (A Guide to Bee-keeping). Pozsony, Leipzig, 1773

that a colony feeds 5000 drones. Then, in July or August, when there is less nectar available and no further swarming is expected the colony expels the drones, or as Shakespeare puts it, they are delivered to the executioners, the workers stab them to death with their stings. These workers will not die as they can withdraw their stings from the chitin-covered scaly bodies of the drones—unlike the soft skin of humans.

Nectar, Flowers and Bee Plants

In Central Europe, thus also in Hungary, we know of about 800 plants visited by bees. Among them are the hermaphrodites, which have stamens and pistils in the same flower and which are pollinated by insects, in a very significant number of cases by bees. The bees' services are reciprocated with food-nectar and pollen—mainly from these plants.

Plants need suitable soil, water, air, sunshine and chlorophyl for photosynthesis. Solar energy accumulates in plants in the form of starch, sugar, tissue and fibre.

The elements from which plants are built up are carried by plant fluids through the tissues. This is how sugars and other materials get to the nectar glands and hairs where they will be available to the bees.

It is very important that a bee can reach this nectar with its proboscis and that the nectar contains a high enough proportion of sugar to make it worth collecting and which has not yet dried up.

Availability depends on the structure of flowers, which differs widely from species to species, and on the location of the hairs and nectary.

The main parts of a flower are the stem, receptacle, ovary, nectary, style, sepals, anthers, stigma, and petals—the latter being responsible for the characteristic colour of the flower. The stigma, style and ovary form the female reproductive organ, whereas anthers and pollen constitute the male equivalent.

Nectar plants: poppy (Papaver erraticum). Drawing from the *Vollständiges Kräuterbuch* by Adami Loniceri. Ulm, 1737

Anthers produce pollen in abundance which, like the number of drones in a strong colony, seems superfluous. In the case of certain species some of the pollen is even sterile; its only use is to feed pollinating insects. The germ of the pollen is vital to the plant for ensuring the propagation of the species. Plants lure insects firstly by offering nectar and pollen but also by their colour, scent and their various shapes. When bees or other insects take pollen from the anthers to the stigma, the pollen will germinate there and the germ will proceed through the style into the ovary. In this way it is fertilized and the development of seeds is started.

The bee may suck up nectar in exchange. The contents of one nectary is not enough, however, to fill its honey sac. A forager may visit fifteen to twenty flowers on a single trip taking along the pollen from one flower to the stigma of another. Some flowers prevent their own pollen from fertilizing themselves either by rejecting their own pollen or by ripening the stigma later than the pollen. Such flowers continue producing nectar after the anthers have been emptied, so that insects should not stop visiting them. The forager takes pollen along on its hairy body. In the case of labiates, for example, where one of the anthers on the two filaments is rudimentary and looks like a little shovel, the process is as follows: The bee alights on the rudimentary anther which bends under its weight. This causes the other filament to rise like the opposite arm of a two-armed balance, and pour its contents of pollen on the bee's head. Pollen from other flowers will again stick to the bee when it puts its head into the flower. From yet other species, pollen is collected on the hairs of the forager's belly while it is sucking up nectar. When collecting from compositae, like the sunflower, the bee is practically bathing in anther-dust, and when it is working on the catkins of a willow it is covered in a shower of pollen.

When a flower is fertilized it stops the secretion of nectar and withers away. There are red flowers whose colour will change once they are fertilized. Such flowers are only visited by bees as long as they are red.

The bee-keepers' direct income from selling honey, beeswax, propolis, bee colonies, queens, pollen and bee poison is at least ten to fifteen times outstripped by the profit to the national economy reaped from the pollination of fruit-trees and various field crops.

When pollinating certain plants it must be taken into consideration that flowers must be visited more than once by the bees to ensure high-quality fruit or crops. For example, apple blossom needs 15 visits, sunflowers 6 and melon flowers 24 visits.

The co-ordination of agricultural production with the activities of bees can be based on data like the following: the proper pollination of one hectar of orchards (e.g. gooseberry, red currants and apricots which are in blossom at the end of March and early April) takes 4 to 5 colonies. A similar number of colonies are enough for one hectar of cherry orchards blossoming between the 10th of April and the 10th of May, and for sour- or morello-cherry trees which are in blossom a few days later. Apple orchards which blossom from the end of April until about the 10th of May, require no more than 3 to 4 colonies per hectare.

Raspberry bushes have an excellent yield from the 10th of May up to the end of June, while black currants and Beszterce plums are similarly productive, blossoming simultaneously with the raspberries, and at the same time acacia groves are in blossom and quince trees also produce good amounts of nectar.

Two or three colonies are enough to significantly increase the crop of several cultivated plants like rape, (flowering between the 20th of April and the 20th of May) white mustard, (between the 15th of May and the 5th of June) white clover (between the 25th of June and the 5th of August) and sunflowers (between the 15th of July and the end of August).

Forest trees like linden and willows as well as acacias yield substantial amounts of nectar and pollen.

Of all the bee plants in Hungary, the acacia is the most important. From one hectar of acacia forest bees may take home as much as 1700 kilos of nectar depending on the soil, weather conditions, sunshine and humidity. Continuous aca-

Nectar plants: cherry-tree (Prunus avium). Drawing from the *Vollständiges Kräuterbuch by* Adami Loniceri. Ulm, 1737

Nectar plants: raspberry (Rubus). Drawing from the *Vollständiges Kräuterbuch* by Adami Loniceri. Ulm, 1737

cia blossoming in Hungary may mean an increase of 10 to 50 kilos in weight per colony during one blossoming period. It is very important that the colony is strong by the time the acacias are in blossom. For a large hive this means 50–80,000 bees of which foragers account for 50–60%. One acacia flower holds 2 mg nectar with a sugar content of 62%.

As mentioned in the previous chapter, one bee can take home 2 mg of nectar in its honey sac on one occasion. The sugar content of ripe acacia honey is around 82%. Accordingly, to produce 1 kg of honey, bees have to cover the distance between the flowers and the hive 75–80,000 times. A forager makes 20 to 35 trips a day, depending on how far the flowers are from the hive.

Acacia trees blossom best on warm, loose soils. In Europe they were introduced early in the eighteenth century, although in Hungary a little later—to bind the sand and give protection against the wind. In addition to these benefits, as with all papilionaceae, nitrogen accumulates at the roots of acacia trees improving the soil and making it suitable for the plantation of, for example, robur trees, and in certain conditions, even for growing field crops.

Bee-keepers call the period of acacia blossoming "main flow", when the bees produce honey which can be taken and put on the market. Honey collected from flowers of the same or different species, flowering not continuously but one after the other, is called "sokhordású" (multiflow).

The Hungarian Research Institute for Forestry carries out research into the potential yield of honey from trees and shrubs in its arboreta at Kámon, Püspökladány and Gödöllő. In Bajti, a collection of various acacias has been set up with the help of foreign research institutes. The aim of this research work is to extend the period of acacia blossoming by propagating varieties which blossom early and late in order to improve the pasture for bees. Another subject of experiment is the possibility of utilizing honey-yielding trees for other purposes. Regrettably acacia trees grow comparatively slowly and are not valuable for their wood. This will very probably lead to the decrease of the 272 thousand hectares under acacia forest today, to about 235 thousand hectares by the year 2000. The effects of this will have to be offset by planting whatever offers better potential for honey, and which flowers for three more weeks. With this aim in mind, the Research Institute for Forestry, supported by the National Enterprise of Apicultural Co-operatives, keeps 850 plants under observation.

The improvement of bee pastures can primarily be carried out in forests, as the spraying of fruit trees and other cultivated nectar plants with insecticides poses increasing threats to apiculture. Herbicides eradicate wild plants and pesticides exterminate insects. The best method seems to be to use bees for the pollination of plants. This can be done by co-ordinating large-scale farming and large-scale bee-keeping. The compulsory notification of spraying is of great help to small apiaries but a method of taking the bees away from the dangerous areas quickly by truck is yet to be found.

Zoltán Faluba, a well-known expert in bee-keeping, published some data regarding pollination by bees. On the Bábolna State Farm, for example, foxtail clover fields yielded 168 kilos of seeds per hectare within a radius of 200–300 metres of the apiary. The corresponding figure for more distant areas was not more than 90 kilos. In the fields of the Farád agricultural co-operative, foxtail clover seed yields increased by 120 kg/hectare as a result of the activities of bees.

Nectar plants: dandelion (Taraxacum officinale). Drawing from the *Vollständiges Kräuterbuch* by Adami Loniceri. Ulm, 1737

The National Joint Enterprise of Apicultural Co-operative also sponsored research into pollination. The team, bearing the name of Sámuel Tessedik and consisting of farm employees assisted by experts used bees for pollination. On the basis of a four-year survey they established that the planned pollinating activities of bees gave an additional yield worth 3,000 million forints annually from 1977 to 1980.

Up to now we have only discussed nectar and pollen-yielding plants, although important constituents for honey are provided by plants producing honeydew. Honeydew is the material collected by bees from the leaves and stems of certain plants. The fluid so called is either secreted by the plant or is pumped out by certain insects—most often by plant lice, who digest the part of the sap needed by them and re-secrete the rest, as a sweet liquid. The bees only suck up these droplets of honeydew if they contain enough moisture.

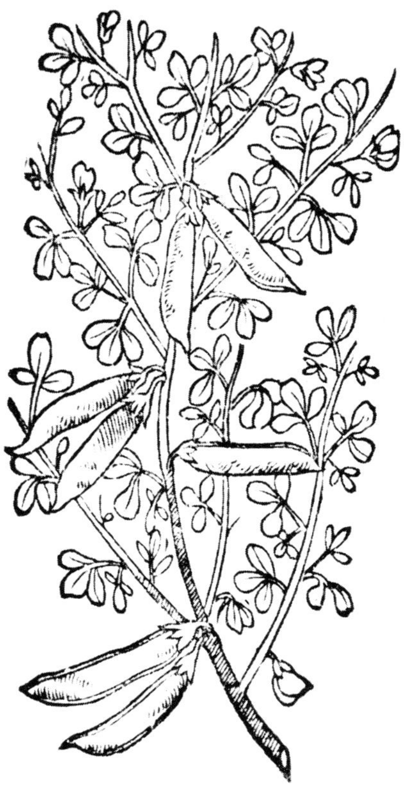

Nectar plants: acacia (Acacia, Robinia pseudoacacia). Drawing from the *Vollständiges Kräuterbuch* by Adami Loniceri. Ulm, 1737

The most important such plants are:

—pinaceae, especially Norwegian spruce, which is used primarily as building timber, Scotch fir, larch, fir and juniper have a rich yield of honeydew. In Germany, Austria and Switzerland these species of trees produce the bulk of constituents for honey together with other plants such as

—several maple varieties—from which both nectar and pollen are collected by bees—,

—poplars and birches,

—varieties of oak and beech and

—chestnut groves.

The bee pasture

One of the most important prerequisites for successful bee-keeping is a well-chosen and cleverly utilized bee pasture where foragers can collect sufficient quantities of nectar and pollen. The most prized are those where plants yielding a lot of nectar occur in large numbers. It is especially desirable for flowers of the same species to cover adjoining fields over a territory which can be covered by the bees, i.e. within a radius of 2.5 to 3 kilometres. When collecting nectar, a forager consumes about 1.5 mg of honey per kilometre, i.e. 7.5% of its total load (20 mg). Long distances may take 5, 10 or even 15% more time, which in turn will reduce the number of trips the bee can make a day. When choosing a place for one's hives this should be taken into consideration. Bees look for flowers whose scent they like and these are usually found pleasing by humans too. This attribute can be made use of by the bee-keeper if he wants his bees to collect tasty, marketable honey from a certain species of flower, or aims at the pollination of some commercial crop. On such occasions he will soak the chosen flower in the water supply or the syrup he uses for feeding the bees. The foragers will look for the same scent when flying over the pasture, as they are loyal to the nectar they have taken a liking to.

In addition to pathogens, parasites, acarine mites, mice, death's-head hawk moths and sugar birds, etc. chemical pesticides are an enemy of bees. Herbicides wipe out and restrict to ever decreasing areas those continuously flowering weeds, especially the ones which flower early in the spring, in the forests, on railway embankments and on the banks of ditches. They are vital to bee colonies and cannot be properly substituted. It is very important that a colony is strong in time for the pollination of orchards when, considering the amount of honey available at the time of acacia blossoming, the colony's population should be at its most numerous. After that the number of bees in the hive may decrease as a time follows when there may not be enough nectar even to feed themselves.

Besides acacia forests, other less important bee pastures should also be considered. From the total forest area of Hungary nectar-bearing trees account for the following proportions:

	Per cent	Thousand ha.
Acacia	21.6	272
Linden	0.8	8
Maple	0.6	
Willow	1.3	13
Elm	0.5	
Forest fruits	0.1	

What the bee-keeper wants to know is the time and duration of flowering, the density of the mass of flowers and how eagerly or not the bees visit them. In the case of trees the rate of growth, feeding value and fruit value are also of indirect interest to him.

For migrating bee-keepers, beginners, and those whose job it is to improve bee pastures, it is important to know the quantities of nectar produced by only one plant and the amount that can be collected by the bees from one hectare of that plant growing in good natural conditions.

	Kilogram/hectare (the peak amount)
Acacia	192–496
outside Hungary was	
Irrigated lucern left for seed production (Medicago sativa)	320
Sunflower (Helianthus)	43
Wound-wort (Stachys)	60
White clover (Trifolium repens)	95
Thistle (Cirsium canum)	105
Common viper's-bugloss (Echium vulgare)	400
Sanfoin (Onobrychis viciifolia)	120
Various willows (Salicaceae)	145
Phacelia tanacetifolia	990
White melilot (Melilotus altissimus)	610
Small-leaved linden (Tilia cordata)	920
(foreign datum)	
Sage (Salvia aethipis)	650
Alsike clover (Trifolium hybridum)	120
Coriander (Coriandrum sativum)	500
Epilobium (Epilobium lanceolatum)	610 (on wet soil)
Yellow melilot (Melilotus italicus)	200
Spurge (Euphorbia lathyris)	26
Common milkweed (Asclepias syriace)	800
Vetch (Vicia)	90

Keeping Bees

Is it worthwhile keeping bees?
We can safely say YES, it pays well to keep bees. In each of the past three years five times as much honey was produced in Hungary as fifty years previously. In the 1930s honey was cheaper than sugar. Today it costs twice as much.

In 1843, the guild-master general of the Hungarian Honeycake Makers' Guild described in his report sent to the directorate of the National Industrial Association (Lajos Kossuth and Count Lajos Batthyány) that bee-keeping was the most useful agricultural activity, as it scarcely required any land and bees could be multiplied almost limitlessly as all the trees and meadows blossomed and flowered for them; if the bees did not collect honey it would only be wasted.

We can go back even further into the past. The apiarist Győző Handerla wrote in his book in 1794:

Those "who can calculate the profits of a hundred sheep over seven years—deducting the loss of dead animals, the cost of keeping them and the payment to the shepherd—as being six to seven hundred forints," and later: "... I promise that whoever treats bees according to the instructions in this booklet will have one thousand and fifty (forints) from one hundred queens, that is skeps, after seven years, and I vow that it will come true."

Obviously every book written on apiculture stresses the profitability of bee-keeping and the success resulting from the application of proper methods. It can also be learned from any book on modern bee-keeping that we should not be afraid of bees. Beginners should protect their faces with caps and bee-veils, and their hands

Jakob Glatz: *Die Bilderwelt.* Vienna, 1811. Illustration: examination of skeps; in the corner there are a worker, a drone and the queen

with gloves, tie a string around the bottom of their trouser legs and generally dress so that the bees cannot get at their skin. An experienced apiarist, on the other hand, who has already made friends with the bees will need much less protection. He knows when, and with what careful calm the bees are to be approached, and will not panic if stung once or twice. It is expedient to remove the sting from the wound quickly so that the painful itching will stop as soon as possible. Smoke and water may also be used to give protection from the stinging mood of bees.

The biggest investment when setting up an apiary these days is the purchase of hives. Before the First World War the so-called national hive was in use. The bee-master had access to the combs by opening a door at the back. The combs were placed in two tiers, one above the other, and the bee-keeper had to take out the whole row if he wanted to examine the frame at the front. Today, the use of top-opening hives is predominant, from which any frame can be taken out very simply with a pair of frame tongs. A more advanced version of this is the multiple-storey hive, where the dwelling place for bees can be augmented by more than one storey. This enables the multiplication of the number of frames, so that the room allowed for incubation is not more than two storeys, whereas the rest, separated by a queen excluder, serves for the storage of honey. Workers can negotiate the openings of the queen excluder without any difficulty, but the queen, with her larger body, has to stay within the space for incubation. The combs in the supers can also be used for the production of comb honey. In smaller frames, of say 100 by 150 mm, virgin combs can be produced. This is another method of preparing comb honey when the combs which fill a normal frame are cut into pieces and are then placed directly in glass jars which are then filled with extracted honey. Both section honey and chunk honey are much more valuable than traditional extracted honey.

In most cases, however, the bee-keeper puts comb foundations, made of beeswax, in the frames of the supers to spare the bees the work of producing wax. To secrete one kilo of beeswax, bees need about as much food as for the production of six to eight kilos of honey. The wax necessary for covering the cells is prepared by the bees anyway. The cappings, removed from the combs with an uncapping knife before extraction, are pure, new beeswax.

Hives are made of boards which are well insulated yet enable necessary respiration. Hive walls can also be made of straw reinforced with laths. The latter is cheaper, but can be holed by woodpeckers or mice and is less simple to keep clean.

The size of a hive depends on that of the colony, the brood, the necessary reserves and the room required by the honey to be taken away and extracted. The bigger the hive, the bigger the colony that can be developed in it.

The swarming impulse, triggered by overcrowding, will be felt sooner by bees kept in a small hive. It should not be forgotten that a lot of space is required for the ripening of liquid honey when there is an ample flow. For acacia flows, when large quantities are collected within a short period, large hives are preferable. On the other hand, when the hives are surrounded by a mixed pasture, where plants are flowering almost continuously, small hives may do, as the frames of filled honeycombs can be taken out regularly for extraction. For migrating bees bigger hives are more economical as the bees are taken to pastures of abundant flow, since the

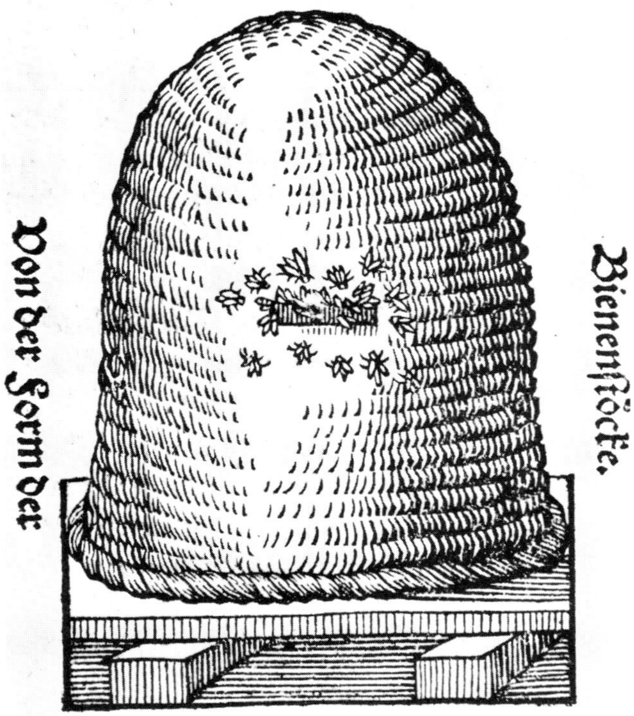

The picture of a hive from *Das neue Bienen Büchlein* by Picus. Pozsony, 1794

costs of freight, loading and staying in various places would otherwise make it unprofitable.

Lots of practical information about keeping bees can be found in the books listed in the Bibliography at the end of this book. Let us rather dwell on the old, simple methods of rural people, still in use today, and perhaps also of interest to experienced and practised apiarists.

Apiaries and skeps in the country

Bees require very little room. Drawings and illustrations in books written hundreds of years ago show apiaries located on the fringes of villages: a tiny square walled garden. Bees lived there in skeps occupying two tiers of shelves along the inner side of the walls. A little door led into the bee garden from the east. The middle of the apiary was left empty for the bees to fly in and out. The high walls were covered with a roof to protect the skeps.

György Handerla kept bees in Nyitra County at the end of the eighteenth century. Let us quote him again: The bee garden should be in a valley among little mountains and hills, yet not in a place where it is in the shade for a long time, or where the hills keep either the morning or the evening sun from the bees... The skeps should be turned towards the sun, there should be neither shrubs nor trees in the way of the bees as they fly out, and the bee-keeper should clean the area around the skeps fortnightly and kill ants with hot water. It is also important that bees enjoying themselves outside can fly back without difficulty."

Another type of apiary found in Zemplén County but also used in other parts of Hungary, is simply a wall or hedge facing east-west with a gabled roof under which the skeps stood in two or sometimes in three tiers with their entrances facing south-east. Such apiaries were set up within a village near the owner's house, or the southern, windowless wall of a house served, together with its roof, as the apiary's wall.

In several Hungarian villages there were 2.5–3 m wide wooden houses on the outside of which stood the skeps, and later, the hives.

Drone trap made of wire-mesh and fastened to a rectangular board. It was mounted on the "mouth" of the skep when the bee-keeper wanted to diminish swarming or prevent further consumption of the honey collected. Found in Komádi, Bihar County. Ethnographical Museum, Budapest

A smoker from Picus's *Das neue Bienen-Büchlein.* Pozsony, 1944.

Behind the bees' dwelling place there was enough room left for tools, spare skeps and hives, and sometimes even a couch or bed was kept there for the elderly bee-keeper to have a rest after work was done, or to sleep on a warm summer's night.

The multiple-storey hives used today are usually kept in the open where they stand on legs in rows. This is the best way to gain access to the frames of these top-opening hives.

For centuries, up to the beginning of the twentieth century, and in exceptional cases even today, skeps were made of tough straw in cylindrical form, tapering away at the top. Some had handles to make lifting easier and there were also angular skeps whose entrance was ornamented with a wolf's head, and a "wolf's throat," so that according to popular belief, the bees would be savage. In other places the skeps were made by winding wicker round a willow bush, dividing it into several long twigs and then smearing it with mud and cattle dung. In marshy regions rushes were also used. We know of bee-cases made of board where a door on the side opposite the entrance offered a view into the lives of the inhabitants. (The skeps used in the various regions are shown on pages 61–64.)

Some incomplete but still useful descriptions of one-time apiaries may be of interest. "A little flower-garden in which there are bees in a skep" (1601). "Five hives of bees in the vineyard of the flower-garden" (1631). A few years later the apiary of Horhy Castle was described as follows: "Opposite the gate of the castle there is a wooden fence... with apricot, sour-cherry, cherry, hazelnut trees within, and 34 hives of bees with 5 empty hives." And finally a note from Sárospatak in 1634: "In a garden of almonds there are two Bienenhofs* containing 38 hives of bees and 13 empty hives."

The reason why so many empty hives are mentioned in the descriptions of apiaries is that these notes were made early in spring when empty skeps of colonies killed with sulphur fumes in the autumn had not yet been filled with new swarms. The killing of bees and the harvesting of their honey took place as follows: The bee-keeper dug a hole in the ground, put sulphur paper into it, set it alight and put the skep of bees on the top. The bees got dizzy and fell into the hole. Then the bee-keeper pulled the sticks which supported the combs out of the skep and, by hitting the edge of it a few times, emptied its contents into a drum. This was ordinary practice even fifty to fifty-five years ago. People were slow to realize that it was worth saving the "bugs", driving them out of the skep by drumming on the sides; or if the queen had disappeared, by separating the bees so that they would beg to be let in by other colonies. If they take enough honey along they are usually allowed in.

Wooden box for finding bees: a small partitioned chest with a sliding lid and a hole on one of the lids. Collected by Dr. Béla Gunda in Domokos, Szolnok County. Ethnographical Museum, Budapest

* Square bee-yards with shelves on the inner side of the fence for the hives. The usual type of apiary in Transylvania in those days.

Before the turn of the century such skeps of honey were often bought by honeycake makers, but apiarists kept some for themselves, carefully cutting out the intact pieces of comb to sell as comb honey. Another practice was to put the combs into a cotton bag for pressing, or to make a miniature wine-press, like the one shown in one of the illustrations.

After the First World War the overwhelming majority of bee-keepers kept their bees in hives, and used the little honey they had in skeps for baking and consumption by their own household.

The bee-keeper's tools and appliances

Around St. Joseph's Day (the 19th of March) when bees regularly fly out of the hive and the water consumption of the colony is on the increase, bee-keepers used to pour water into a wooden trough and put some pieces of wood into it. Bees, whose weight is about a tenth of a gram, could safely alight on the floating pieces of wood and take their fill of water. The brood particularly needs a lot of water. A recent method of supplying water is to trickle the water continuously onto a slanting surface.

The bee-keeper also needs a long ladder to remove swarms which have settled in high places, although it is better not to have very high trees around the apiary so that bees will choose low-lying places for gathering and resting. From such places it is easier to sweep them into a vessel prepared in advance or, temporarily, into a skep. First swarms particularly like to settle down in the immediate vicinity of the hive as they leave together with the old queen. Once a swarm has been caught it is best if the bees are

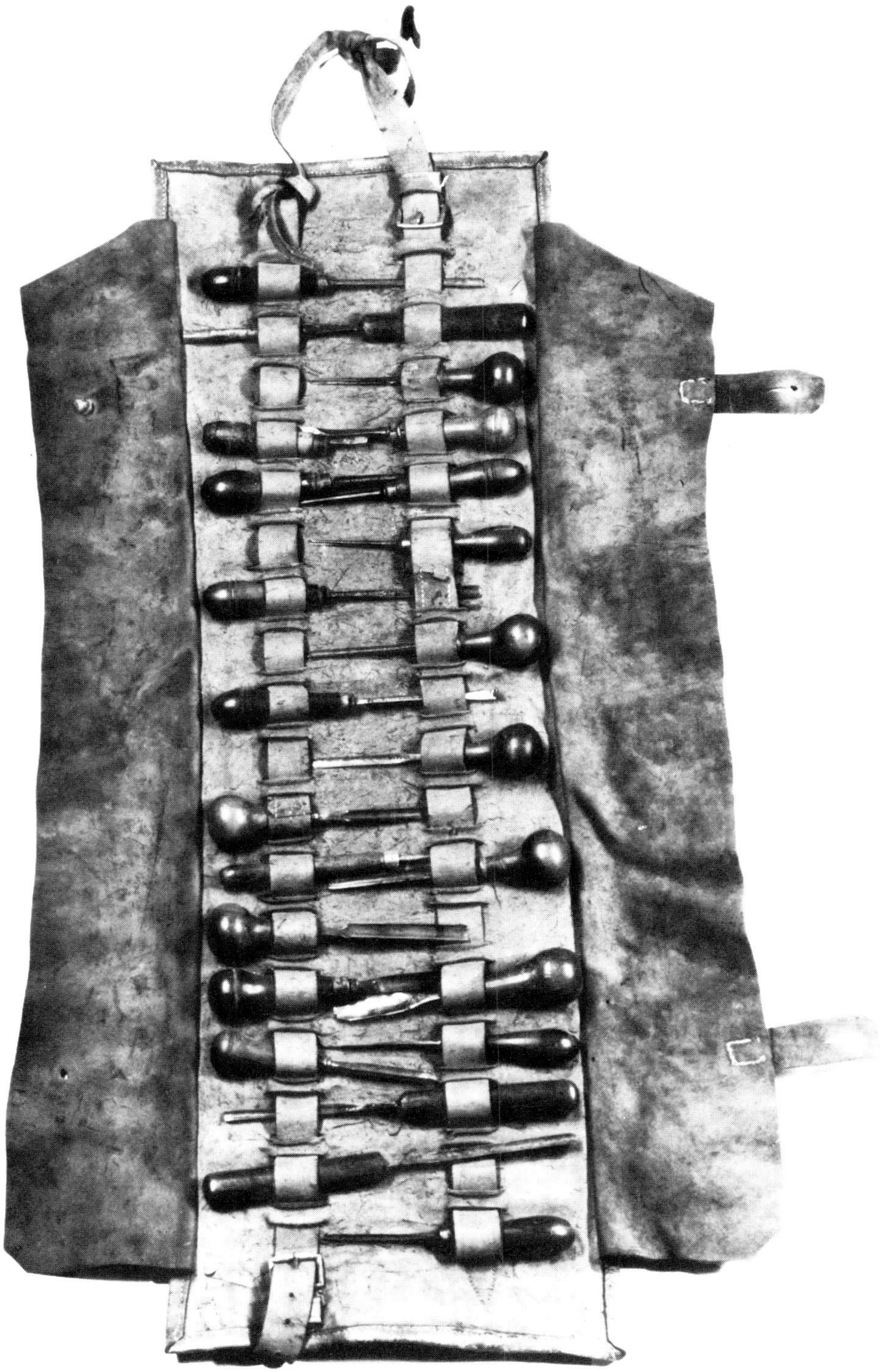

Imre Beliczay's set of carving tools. Private collection

immediately put into their new place which has been fitted out with one or two honey- and pollen-combs as well as with frames with comb foundations. That is, before swarming, the bees take their fill of honey which they will be glad to deposit in their new hive.

As mentioned above, smoke is usually used to overpower bees, and for this purpose several types of smokers are employed. A few of them can be seen in the pictures.

It may also prove useful to have something to squirt robber bees with to drive them away.

The apiarist who keeps his bees in skeps needs a special curved knife with which he can cut out combs without damaging the rest. When bees live in hives the bee-keeper needs an uncapping knife or fork to remove the caps of the cells before extracting the honey.

For working with skeps a hatchet was also needed. This was used for hitting the sticks which held the combs out of the skeps, after the bees were either doped or had been driven out of the skep.

Nowadays it is easy to examine bees living in top-opening hives by taking out any of the frames. In the days when skeps were used, the bee-keeper was in a much more difficult position. When he found that bees were flying out only seldom or in an unusual way, he turned the skep upside down and looked for the queen among the combs. If he could not find her and

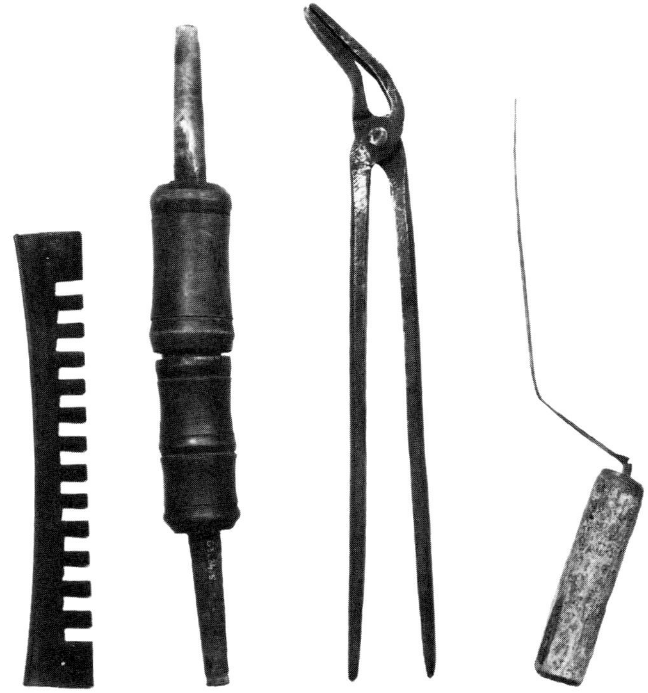

Apiarists protected their bees from mice and death's-head hawk moths by narrowing the entrance. The curved strip of sheet iron which had 6 cm long teeth was mounted on the hive in the autumn and left there until a few days before the acacia flow
A pipe smoker, bee pipe and wooden pipe. Tobacco smoke was blown into the skep through a double tube made of hardwood as a result of which the bees were stunned and it was easy to cut out the combs. Found in Botpalád, Szatmár County.
Large iron tongs ware used for taking the frames out. Size: 26 cm.
The hive was cleaned with a special bee-keeper's knife. Length: 28 cm. Found in Somogy County. Ethnographical Museum, Budapest

"Lat": measuring instrument consisting of 6 interlocking pieces with a lid. Ethnographical Museum, Budapest

there were also other signs indicating that the colony had become queenless, he cut out part of the lower comb and replaced it with a queen cell. The operation required a covered cell in which the queen was already in the pupa stage. The colony usually accepted the queen emerging from such a cell.

A honey extractor, used for harvesting surplus honey, consists of a large cylindrical vessel and comb-holders—baskets—revolving around an axis. As a result of turning it round fast, the centrifugal force removes the honey from the uncapped combs. The first extractor was very probably used and described by Franz Hruska in Austria in 1865. Bee-masters who were deft craftsmen as well, soon made wooden extractors in Hungary, too. It is most important that the honey flowing from the extractor is carefully strained lest fragments of beeswax, bees' legs, wings or other tiny contaminations should get into the final product which can cause rapid crystallization.

Up to the beginning of the Second World War, it was customary in some regions of Hungary to collect dry combs and comb wastes. Once the harvest was over men went all over the country to purchase waxy wastes and sent them home. Those villages which collected beeswax had a communal wax press which was in some cases as high as 15 metres.

Popular beliefs in connection with bees

It was believed in olden times that a colony bought for money would bring no profit, only those colonies exchanged for wheat would develop, swarm and multiply well.

Womenfolk should not be involved in beekeeping lest they put a spell on the bees.

Several customs caught on in order to prevent theft and bad spells. One of them was to tie as many knots in a twist as was the number of the colonies in the apiary. The bee-keeper then touched a skep with each knot in turn, and turned on his heel, on every occasion in front of witnesses. In some places, the entrance to the skep was smeared with mud made with holy water, so that mice, death's-head hawk moths or ants should not have the courage to climb into the skep. Apiaries were surrounded by high fences so that the bees could not have the evil eye cast on them.

To prevent foreign bees from robbing the skep sweepings from the church floor were thrown under it. At other times a stake with a horse's skull was driven into the ground in front of the apiary to turn evil away. Also, blessed willow or other twigs were thrust into the skep.

Sometimes a wolf's larynx was put into the entrance of the skep or the entrance was made in such a way as to look like the open mouth of a wolf.

It was considered useful to pull a piece of red cloth through the entrance of the skep so that the bees would be savage, collect more honey and, if somebody approached them with evil intentions, would protect themselves. It was not desirable on the other hand that they should sting their own master, so the entrance of the skep was smeared with ewe's milk, and white wool which had been soaked in milk, was pulled through it.

To prevent the bees from stinging them, beekeepers urinated on their own hands and surrounded themselves with smoking pitchpine.

They believed they could incite their bees to work even harder by placing an ant-hill under the apiary. (This contradicts the rule that ants are to be killed off in the apiary using hot water, and yet this belief was widely accepted in certain regions.)

At Christmas time there were celebrations of the honey harvest in some parts of the country. People took out bigger pieces of honeycomb from the skep and gave them as gifts to relatives and friends. When returning the honey bowl the friend or relative would give some wheat in exchange which was then to be scattered under the skeps.

The release of bees was celebrated on St. Joseph's Day, the 19th of March. According to popular belief the bee-keeper should not give anyone anything out of his house on that day. The best days for letting the bees out were Wednesday and Thursday when everything could be well prepared in advance and there was time to arrange things afterwards, too.

It was also widespread belief that bees were the bugs of King Solomon, and that one should not use the word usually applied to animals when a bee died but the one reserved for humans. In the trough at the drinking place the bee-master sometimes added a quarter part of wine to the water to strengthen the bees, a few cloves to warm their stomachs and a little camphor oil against colic.

There are also children's games which seem to be connected with honey:

> Honey, honey, yielded honey,
> the blessedness of yielded honey.
> This blessed nectar
> ferments every day,
> if you have a good drink of it,
> it will make you healthy and gay.

It was sung by girls standing in a circle, holding hands who raised and then lowered their hands according to the rhythm. One of them walked around the circle occasionally miming having a drink. Usually this was followed by the dialogue of "asking for a girl's hand" game: "Why are you circling, why are you turning around my house?"

Denomination, Chemical Composition and Properties of Honey

After defining honey in Chapter 1, let us make a little detour and discuss the words honey and bee themselves.

In the opinion of Péter Hajdu, professor of bee-keeping, the part of the Russian scientist, Köppen's theory which is of lasting value, is the discussion of the possibility of a relationship between the Indo-European and Finno-Ugrian languages. Here he tried to define the original home of the Finno-Ugrian peoples. As proof he referred, among other things, to the Iranian origin of the words *méz* (honey) and *méh* (bee). Actually the Hungarian *méz,* Finnish *mesi,* Mordvinian *med,* Cheremissian and Udmurt *mu* are all loan words coming from the Sanskrit *madhu* and the Iranian *madu* and *medhu,* but then this is also where the source of the Latin word *mel* can be found. Mead is called *mesla* in Lappish, and the Finnish equivalent for bee is *mehiläinen,* whereas it is called *meks* in Mordvinian and *mus* in Udmurt and Komi. In the *Vedas* of India a little bee is called *madhukarika.*

From this information and several other loanwords it seems it can only be proved that Iranian peoples lived south of the Ugrian country of origin, in western Siberia and the Volga-Don region. Ancient Hungarians supposedly learned collecting honey there.

Mud-smeared straw skep with wolf's head.
According to popular belief a bee colony
"passing through a wolf's throat"
would be as fierce as a wolf.
Ethnographical Museum, Budapest

Conical skep made according to the ancient method of weaving grape vines around a forked branch and smearing them with cow dung and mud. Height: 72 cm. Ethnographical Museum, Budapest

Bell-shaped skep woven from rushes and smeared with a mixture of cow dung and mud. Diameter: 40 cm. Found in Sonkád, Szabolcs–Szatmár County. Ethnographical Museum, Budapest

Honey-press carved of hard wood.
Height: 81 cm. Found in Tarpa,
Szabolcs–Szatmár County.
Ethnographical Museum, Budapest

Skep carved of willow. Height: 61 cm. Found in Tarpa, Szabolcs–Szatmár County. Ethnographical Museum, Budapest

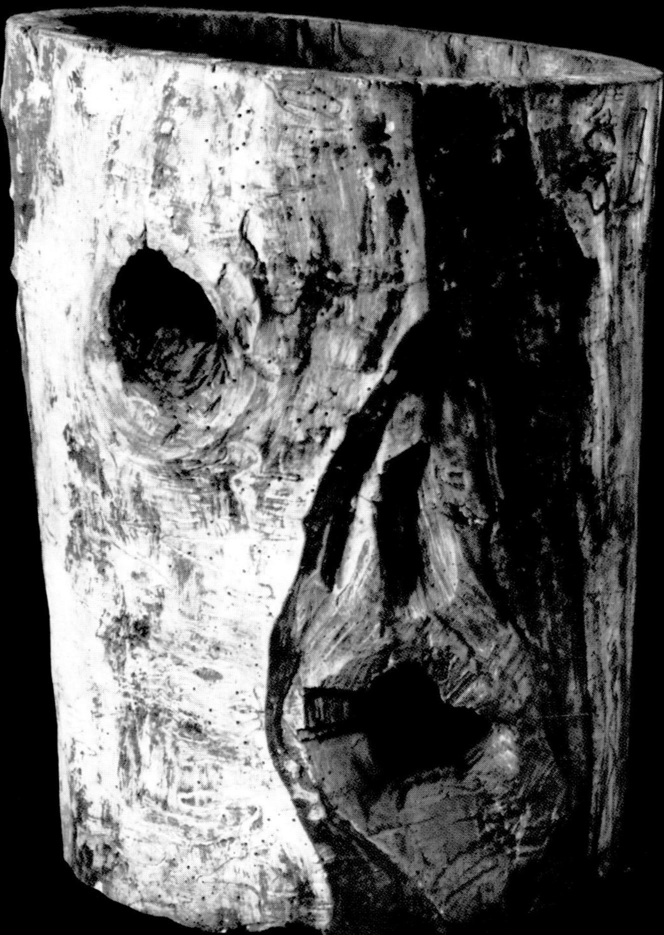

Tup-skep, bee-hive with an oak lid. A tub made by hollowing out a linden trunk; dated 1824, initialled LM. Height: 64 cm. Probably originating from the bee garden of a nobleman. Ethnographical Museum, Budapest

Crustullum forms produced in the Pacatus workshop in the 2nd century A. D. Aquincum Museum, Budapest

Marcus Aurelius and Lucius Verus co-emperors

Danae

Pan and goat

Hercules and the bull of Crete

Mercurius riding a ram

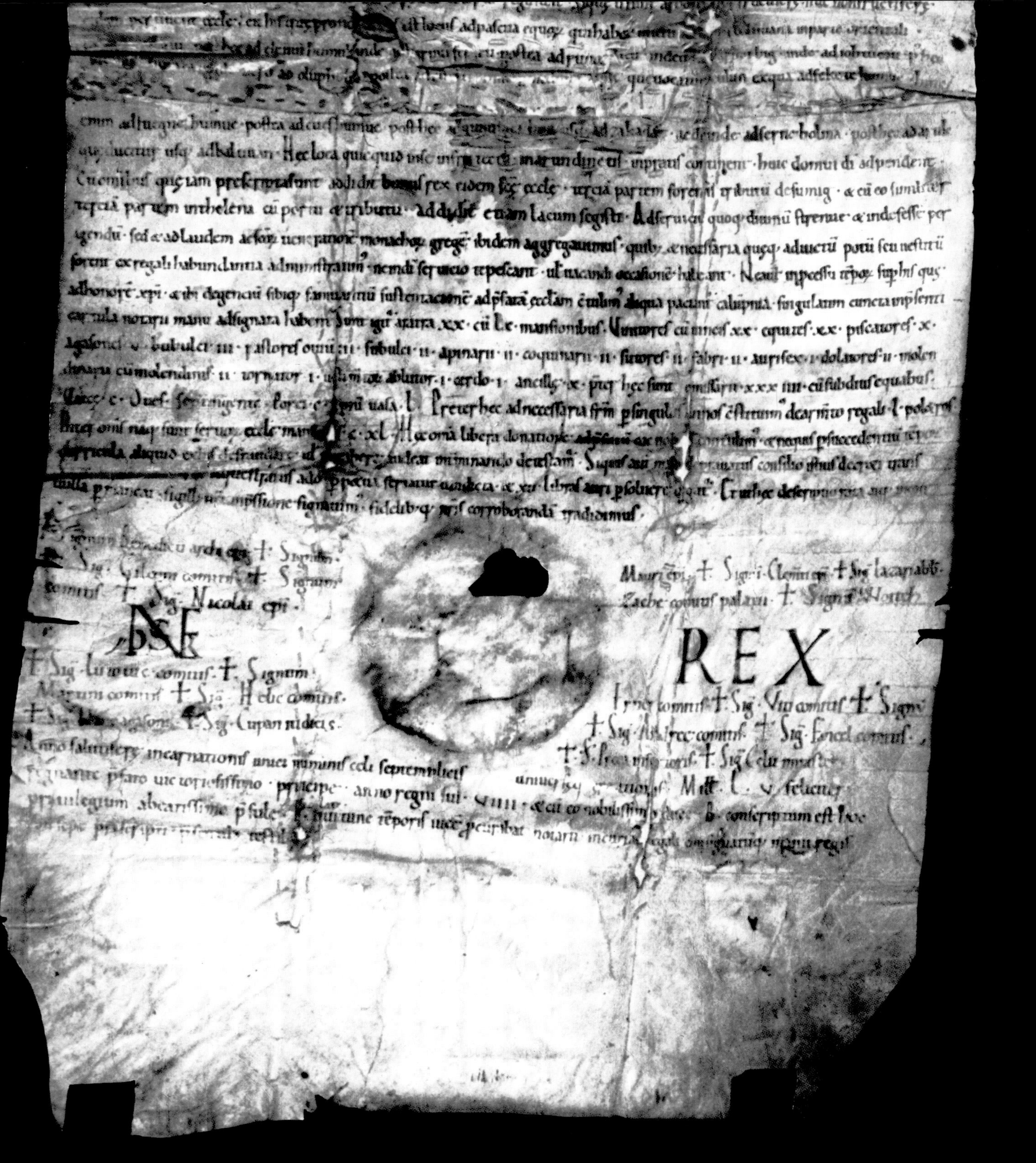

[illegible] ad olimpi [illegible] quę uocatur [illegible] ecquis adsesse [illegible]

enim alsu eque [illegible] postea ad curs [illegible] post hec [illegible] ad [illegible] deinde ad serne holma · post hec [illegible]

[illegible] usque ad bal [illegible] · Hec loca quicquid in se infra terrę in arundine uel in pratis continent · huic domui di adpendent ·

[illegible] que iam prescripta sunt · addidit [illegible] rex eidem scę ecclę · terciam partem forensis tributi de sumig · et cum eo similiter

terciam partem in thelena cum portu et tributu · addidit etiam lacum segistr · Ad seruicium quoque diuinum strenue et indefesse per

agendum · sed et ad laudem [illegible] monachorum gregem ibidem aggregauimus · quibus et necessaria queque ad uictum potum seu uestitum

forent ex regali habundantia administrauimus · ne in di seruicio tepescant · uel uacandi occasionem habeant · Ne autem in processu temporum superbis quis

ad honorem xpi et ibi degencium sibique famulantium sustentacionem ad prefatam ecclesiam [illegible] aliqua paciant calumpnia · singulatim cuncta in presenti

cartula notarii manu adsignata habent · Sunt igitur aratra xx · cum l · x · mansionibus · Uinitores cum uineis xx · equites · xx · piscatores · x ·

agasones · u · bubulci · iii · pastores ouium · ii · subulci · ii · apiarii · ii · coquinarii · ii · sutores · ii · fabri · ii · aurifex · i · dolatores · ii · molen

dinarii cum molendinis · ii · tornator · i · [illegible] · i · cerdo · i · ancillę · x · preter hec sunt [illegible] xxx · iiii · cum subditis equabus ·

[illegible] · c · oues · sexcentę · [illegible] · l · Preter hec ad necessaria fratrum per singulos annos [illegible] regalis · l · [illegible]

[illegible] omnis [illegible] sunt seruorum ecclę [illegible] · c · xl · Hec omnia libera donatione [illegible] ex nostro [illegible] successorum temporum

[illegible] aliquid ex his defraudare uel [illegible] minuendo deuastare · Si quis autem [illegible] consilio [illegible]

[illegible] ad [illegible] xii · libras auri persoluere [illegible] · Ut autem hec [illegible]

[illegible] sigilli nostri impressione signauimus · fidelibusque nostris corroborandam tradidimus ·

Signum [illegible] archiepi · ✝ · Signum [illegible]

Sig · [illegible] comitis · ✝ · Signum [illegible]

comitis · ✝ · Sig · Nicolai epi ·

[illegible]

✝ · Sig · [illegible] comitis · ✝ · Signum

[illegible] comitis ✝ · Sig · [illegible] comitis ·

✝ · Sig · [illegible] · ✝ · Sig · [illegible]

Mauricii [illegible] ✝ · Sig · [illegible] ✝ · Sig · [illegible] abbatis ·

[illegible] comitis palatini · ✝ · Sig · [illegible]

REX

[illegible] comitis · ✝ · Sig · [illegible] comitis · ✝ · Signum

✝ · Sig · [illegible] comitis · ✝ · Sig · [illegible] comitis ·

✝ · S · [illegible] · ✝ · Sig · [illegible]

Anno salutiferę incarnationis [illegible] M · LXXV · feliciter ·

regnante [illegible] uictoriosissimo · principe · anno regni sui · [illegible] et cum eo nobilissimo [illegible] conscriptum est hoc

priuilegium [illegible] · [illegible] temporis [illegible] notarii [illegible] regis

[illegible]

◁ **The deed of foundation of the Tihany Abbey.** ***"Abbeys are to tak tithe from honey and should not be hindered either in the fields, vineyards or fishing or in the keeping of bees."*** **From the Szőlős Manor 12** ***akós*** **(*c.* 144 gallons) of honey had to be delivered to the Abbey every year. Hungarian National Archives, Budapest**

Christ on the cross with the Virgin Mary and Magdalene. Carved honeycake mould. Late 18th century. Kiscelli Museum, Budapest

Virgin Mary with the infant Jesus. Carved honeycake mould. Kiscelli Museum, Budapest

Cock in a flowering field. Carved honeycake mould. Kiscelli Museum, Budapest

Cock among flowers. Carved honeycake mould. Kiscelli Museum, Budapest.

Ornamented sword: its hilt is a hussar, its blade is decorated with foliage and floral patterns. Carved honeycake mould. Kiscelli Museum, Budapest

Babe in swaddling-clothes. Honeycake mould carved of oak. Kiscelli Museum, Budapest

The Hungarian coat of arms,
with the royal crown and imperial
eagle of the Habsburg dynasty,
in a setting of ostrich plumes.
Carved honeycake mould.
Kiscelli Museum, Budapest

The composition of honey

Nectar collected from various flowers and the honeydew taken from other parts of plants will turn into honey of different qualities.

In a hundred kilos of mixed flower honey the following constituents are usually found:

	Kg
Fructose	41,0
Dextrose	34,0
Saccharose (cane sugar)	2,0
Dextrin	1,70
Melezitose and maltose	0,40
Dulcitol	0,30
Other sugars	0,30
Amino acids	0,80
Vitamins (A, B_1, B_2, B_6, C, G, PP, folic acid, etc.)	0,005
Potassium	0,01
Phosphorus	0,03
Copper	0,01
Sodium	0,005
Lime	0,0005
Manganese	0,0006
Iron	0,00006
Sulphur	0,00004
Enzymes	0,0038
Colloids	0,04
Water	17,00
Other non-defined materials	2,395
	100,00

The chemical composition of the various types of honey may differ widely. The proportion of water, which has the greatest influence on the physical properties of the honey, may vary between 15 and 20%, whereas that of fructose may be between 22 and 44%. Dextrose varies between 32 and 49%, and cane sugar, which may be as high as 10% in some flower honeys, can fall to as low as 0.2% after being stored for a long time.

Tiny amounts of scent material and aroma also occur in honey. They cast some light on the origin of the nectar and, together with pollen analysis, can identify the flower from which the bee collected it. The highest proportion of these materials can be found in comb honey; in the process of extracting the honey and making it flow, as in pressing and heating, some of its properties will be lost. Heating primarily affects the colour of the honey—it will be darker as a result of the decomposition of proteins.

It is not unreasonable to put particular emphasis on the sweet taste of honey. It is, indeed, sweeter than cane or beet sugar. If we give cane sugar (called saccharose by the scientist),

100 points for its sweetness, then fructose will get 173 points

grape sugar	74 points
invert sugars	123 points
maltose	32 points
raffinose	23 points
lactose	16 points

That is, the sweetest honeys are those containing a lot of fructose, particularly acacia honey, whose fructose content is at least 42% as against the 34% of an average mixed flower honey.

Honey with a high level of dextrose will crystallize within a short time. This process does not decrease the value of the honey, nor is it an indication of the presence of foreign matters. Some people even have a predilection for "granulated honey".

If crystallization takes place in a glass jar or other packaging, one can reconstitute its original

Hussar on foot in corded pelisse with sword.
Carved honeycake mould. Kiscelli Museum, Budapest

shining, liquid form oneself. The jar of honey should be put into a pot of water heated to 45 °C. Soon the honey will melt along the sides of the jar and should be stirred gently. When all the crystals have disappeared, the jar should be taken out of the pan. It is advisable to cool it quickly afterwards as high temperature affects the colour of honey and weakens its aroma. On the other hand it has the advantage of killing yeast fungi which are introduced into almost all honey by pollen.

Bee-keepers are familiar with the superb fragrance which can be smelt during extraction. The scent comes off the honey in the course of heating. This is why comb honey is most delicious and aromatic in its original concentration and purity.

Honey is classified into three groups according to its origin.

Mihály Csokonai Vitéz. Carved honeycake mould with the dates 1773 and 1883. Déri Museum, Debrecen

The first group consists of honey collected from *one single variety of flowers,* like acacia honey, linden honey, woundwort honey, white clover honey, etc. which is considered the finest. They contain 80 to 90% of honey originating from the variety named or in the case of acacia honey, even more. Before the time of acacia blossoming bee-keepers extract all the honey in the honeycombs so that the bees can take acacia honey into clean, empty cells. Once blossoming is over, all acacia honey is extracted lest it mix with nectar from other species.

Acacia honey smells of acacia blossom, has a light yellow colour, mild taste, and will not crystallize for several months.

White clover honey, which has a very pleasant, mild aroma, is almost as clear as water. It has a moisture content of 16% and will crystallize within one or two months.

Linden or lime honey is yellow, sometimes with a greenish hue, and with the well-defined scent of linden flowers. After a few months it will crystallize and turn greyish-brown.

Spurge honey is dark yellow, almost brown, and has a pleasant, though slightly rough after-taste.

Woundwort honey is as clear as water, it crystallizes quickly turning snow white in the process. It, too, has a slightly granular after-taste.

There is a thorny weed called *butykoró,* in the vicinity of the town of Szentes, which grows on roadsides and the banks of ditches to a height of 30–40 centimetres and whose yellow flowers yield a bright light yellow honey with a pleasant taste reminiscent of malt. In arid summers when the nectar flow was poor it came in very handy to replenish stocks.

The second group of honey is multiflower honey and the third is honeydew honey.

The taste of honey is very complex. Basically we distinguish four main varieties. With the tip of the tongue we sense sweetness, on the two sides behind the tip, saltiness, further behind sourness, on the palate, the back of the tongue bitterness. The last category includes the most subtle and pleasant, the finest tastes. Apart from these we can also perceive metallic, alkaline and stringent tastes. It depends on the tastes and the scents which reach the mucous membranes through our noses, what we perceive as pleasant, and what we like. In the USSR epilobium honey is the favourite whereas in the US clover honey is highly appreciated. Surprisingly, there also are quite a lot of people who prefer buckwheat honey.

As mentioned above the thickness, fluidity and viscosity of honey is also important to the consumer. Slowly flowing honey has high viscosity while liquid honey has low viscosity. The factor which has the greatest influence on the viscosity is the moisture content; even a 1% increase results in considerable thinning. Honey with a high dextrine level tends to be thick while that which contains lots of colloidal material is thinner. Also, honey with a high fructose content will be more fluid than another with the same water content but less fructose.

Acacia honey, for example, will be pleasantly thick and full-bodied even with 16% water. Buckwheat honey will have a similar consistency when containing 18% water.

Temperatures have a similar effect on the thickness of honey. Honey which is thick when kept at 12–14 °C in the winter, will be unpleasantly liquid at 20–22 °C in the summer. It is expedient therefore, to keep the honey jar in the frigidaire during the summer and on the larder or kitchen shelf in the winter.

The fluidity of honey can be decreased by mixing it with butter before consumption (3/10 honey+7/10 butter). Care should be taken, however, as the butter will be rancid in about three days at room temperature so any leftovers should be used within a short time.

Another important property of honey is hygroscopicity. When the relative humidity of the air in the storage room is below 60%, honey will lose some of its water content (and a corresponding percentage of weight). When humidity is more than 60%, honey will absorb some of the moisture from the air.

Hygroscopicity is very important for honeycake makers because it is this property of honey which ensures that their cakes will stay soft for a long time.

Enzymes in honey

Enzymes have a very important role in nature, especially in the triggering and carrying through of certain chemical processes. Honey also contains such enzymes, for example, invertase,

Bee finder: either bees alighting on flowers were taken or their nests were found with them. Carved of cattle horn. Ethnographical Museum, Budapest

which is transferred from the plant, mainly by the bee, to the honey, and transforms cane sugar into dextrose and fructose. The 2 to 6% of cane sugar present in the ripe, extracted honey may decrease to as little as 0.2 to 2% during the period of storage. Diastase, on the other hand, turns starch into sugar. When the honeycake dough is set aside for fermentation, some of the flour which is mixed with the honey will be transformed into sugar. Other enzymes, some of which also occur in the human saliva, stomach and small intestine, are also present in honey. This is why honey can assist a person's bodily functions, too.

Enzymes are sensitive to heat. Temperatures over 45 °C will stop or at least diminish their capability for catalyzing.

Ensuring the quality of honey

The quality of the honey must meet the requirements of Hungarian and international standards. The Hungarian Standard includes several regulations which were included in foreign standards only later, for example, that only products prepared by honeybees can be termed honey. The Hungarian Standard strictly forbids changing the colour of the honey artificially. Neither is it permitted to change the weight of honey by the addition of water, invert sugar, or any other foreign matter. It is also forbidden to falsify or conceal the data concerning the origin and/or the quality of the honey (Hungarian Standard No. MSz 6950 1–72).

According to the method of treatment, the Standard only lists comb honey, extracted honey and pressed honey. The classification of the honey must be indicated on its packaging. First class honey can be called acacia, linden, lavender or mixed flower honey, whereas second class honey can only be presented simply as honey. The name may indicate the geographical region where the honey has come from and may also include a remark referring to some special properties, e.g. creamed. The honey must not contain any contamination or have any unusual taste, smell or aroma.

Mould for honeycake plate with coat of arms surrounded by an Austrian oak and blossoming branch. Inscription: *"Pázmándy Gyula, Debreczen"*. Déri Museum, Debrecen

For honey originating from the flowers of one species, the Standard prescribes the colour, taste smell and aroma as well as the type and quantity of pollen that it is allowed to contain. In 100 g of acacia honey, for instance, there should be 30 grains of pollen.

The quality of the various types of honey is jointly guaranteed by Hungaronektár (the company that markets it) and Monimpex (the Hungarian Foreign Trading Company in charge of its export). Each batch of honey is analyzed on arrival and its quality established in the laboratory. No honey at variation with the prescribed Standard can be marketed.

The provisions of the Standard also cover the conditions under which honey is produced, processed, stored, packed, transported, sampled. For example, only such vessels can be used whose material or coating cannot be broken down by honey to such an extent that the resulting chemical changes will render the honey harmful to human health.

The Standard also includes a list of types of honey in the order of its tendency to crystallization.

It is the duty of the Hungarian veterinary service to carry out research into the prevention of bee diseases and so to arrest the spread of any infection. In this way the spread of bee diseases, either within Hungary or through export, can be stemmed.

Checks are also made in veterinary laboratories to ensure that the honey is absolutely free of insecticides, herbicides or fertilizers. Acacia honey is among the best in this respect too; acacia forests are never sprayed or fertilized. Meanwhile, the research for sprays which destroy orchard pests but which cause no harm to bees or humans, continues.

The Effects of Honey and Other Apicultural Products on Health

After covering the military and other uses of honey associated with cults in previous chapters, let us now relate its history of many thousand years from the point of view of doctors and people who have wished to keep their bodies healthy.

In the museum of archaeology in Philadelphia (Pa.) there is a stone slab inscribed with the prescriptions of a Sumerian doctor each including honey among its ingredients. In ancient Mesopotamia honey was quite often given to convalescent patients as a roborant.

The most remarkable record, however, of the use of honey as a medicine, is a treasured Egyptian papyrus scroll kept in a Leipzig museum. It was discovered by G. Ebers who gave its complete translation in his book which appeared in 1875. The period to which the scroll dates back is still debated. In Ebers's opinion it was written in 1550 B.C. during the rule of Pharaoh Amenhotep, whereas I. Dümichen argues that it must have come into being in the first dynasty, sometime during the period 2400–2700 B.C. In his study he wrote that the scroll was more than 5300 years old. The relic was a summary of the experiences of Egyptian doctors. Honey was used for aiding digestion and also as an ingredient of ointments for healing wounds and curing boils. Among the prescriptions there is also a prophylactic against bee stings which must have produced the desired result, its smell being repellent to bees.

According to the book on bee-keeping by the

Carthaginian Mago (fourth century B.C.) honey was a popular medicine of the people for both internal and external application.

Hippocrates, the greatest physician of ancient Greece and all the ancient world, held that wine and honey were very important for man, and more importantly that both healthy and sick people should use them in compliance with their natures, at the appropriate time and place.

Plutarch wrote of the deinebriating effect of honey, which is recommended by doctors even today to those who wish to get rid of the habit of drinking too much.

According to Dioscorides, honey has cleansing properties, and of drawing out of bodily fluids, so it can be used for the cleansing of festering and dirty wounds. It has a curative effect on the oral cavity and is a good mouth wash against the diseases of the larynx and the oesophagus.

Emperor Augustus asked Romulus Pollio, who was 102 years old, what he thought had prolonged his life. "Obviously the mead I drink every day," the old man replied.

Pliny mentions that honey-dough, a mixture of honey and flour, which after a few months of fermentation, was placed on the infected area of skin, both as a blistering plaster, and as a skin softener, so that the puss was drawn out. This was known as a home remedy even forty years ago, and was available at honeycake makers'.

In the sixteenth century doctors recommended the consumption of honey to old people and those sensitive to cold, but cautioned the young and choleric against it because honey was supposed to increase bile formation and various passions.

In olden times honeycake slabs were also used for medication: they cured inflammations in the oral cavity with it. They chipped small pieces off the honey slab, baked exclusively of honey and flour, and after dipping them into milk, put them into the inflamed part of the oral cavity. It then slowly crumbled away in the mouth. It had a good effect locally and it improved digestion.

There are many apothecary vessels treasured in museums and old chemist's shops in Hungary, the inscriptions of which show how many kinds of honey preparations were used for curative purposes. E.g. *Mel rosatum* (honey with rose oil), *Mel depuratum* (purified honey), *Mulsa* (mead — Roman), *Hydromel* (mead — French), *Mel pector* (expectorant honey), *Oximel* (acid honey), and *Nectar* (honey diluted with wine). Some of the richly ornamented ceramic apothecary's vessels were made by the Habans (potters of the Anabaptist denomination), who had fled Switzerland and come through Moravia to arrive in Transylvania and Upper Hungary in the sixteenth–seventeenth centuries. Their vessels are usually ornamented in yellow, pink, green and blue against a white, ivory or blue background. In his book which appeared in Pozsony in 1787 under the title *Ó és Új Diaetetica* (Old and New Dietetics), István Mátyus, a doctor, wrote: "In the apothecaries, especially when cane-honey (sugar) was not available in ample quantities, almost a quarter of the medicines consisted of pure honey."

Against what diseases is honey recommended nowadays? The best results can be gained from using it as a preventive measure, i.e. by regular, daily consumption.

Now that for many years there have been a variety of plants from which sugar can be made, honey has been almost totally replaced by sugar in many households. Although in the last thirty years this trend has abated somewhat, even in developed countries annual honey consumption is not more than 300 to 800 g per capita, while sugar consumption, which was around 8–10 kilos at the beginning of our century, has grown to 30–50 kilos.

In little villages in the middle of nowhere, where old traditions survive, there are many people who take one or two spoonfuls of honey every day. In the Soviet Union, N. P. Voyrich observed such old people. According to his notes, Abzeiev lived 117 years, Toshkin 134 and Gunak Gusiev 166 years, thanks to their well functioning hearts and intestines.

Thirty or forty years ago in the USA (Vermont) a doctor, D. C. Jarvis, noticed that there were quite a lot of people doing hard manual labour at the age of 70 and even 80, who were regular consumers of honey. With the assistance of fifty other doctors he researched in thirty-two states for twenty years and published his observations concerning the therapeutic effects of honey. As he observed, honey helps maintain good physical condition and mental alertness, relieves nervous tension and has a sedative effect: in the evening a glass of water with honey ensures a good, deep sleep.

The blood sugar level of people doing hard manual work decreases, phosphates and chlorides leave the body with the urine passed, and productivity diminishes. Marathon runners and cross-country skiers achieve better results when consuming honey during the race.

In addition to old people and those doing tiring physical work, honey can be especially recommended to children and expectant mothers. In Swiss paediatric nursing homes honey is substituted for sugar wherever possible. Doctors place particular emphasis on the appetizing effect of honey resulting most probably from its flavour and fragrance, volatile oils and organic acids. It has also been observed that the number of red corpuscules increased more quickly in the blood of children who took honey regularly than in the blood of the control group.

The phosphate content of honey, the iron compounds and other trace elements, copper, cobalt and folic acid, all further the intake for iron. Zaiss, who made the above statement, was the first modern doctor who prescribed water mixed with honey to children with intestinal complaints. V. Kokas demonstrated as early as the 1930s, that the classic spices of honeycake, cinnamon and cloves, have a stimulating effect

Das neue
Bienen-Büchlein/
Das ist:
ützlicher Unterricht von Bie-
/ woher sie kommen: Wie vielerley
ren seyn; wann und wie sie schwärmen/
auch wie man die fassen und ersprießlichen war-
ten solle/ daß man sie fruchtbarlich
geniessen könne/ etc.

Picus: *Das Neue Bienen-Büchlein.* Pozsony, 1794. Title-page on digestion in a dilution of 1/1,000 and 1/25,000 respectively.

In view of the discovery of the special active ingredients and effects of honey, animal experiments were carried out. In 1968 Prof. János Rigó and Prof. József Sós, principals of the Dietetical Institute of SOTE (Semmelweis Orvostudományi Egyetem=Semmelweis Medical University), observed four groups of rats kept on four different diets. In the course of swimming competitions the performance of the group which had been fed on honey started to improve after the third week, and was twice as good as that of the control groups in the sixth week.

E. Kock, a Frenchman, experimented with frogs. The heart of the test animal which had been stopped, started to beat again within a second after an injection of honey, whereas a cane sugar injection had the same effect only after a much longer time.

The potency of honey as a medicine may prove different in various cases. On the one hand, the sensitivity of patients is different and, on the other, the concentration and the proportions of the active ingredients are also different in the various types of honey.

As a home remedy honey is most often used against colds, mixed into warm milk or linden-blossom tea. To cure a cough it is suggested that a lemon should be boiled for 10 minutes until its peel is soft. It will then give lots of juice and some of the volatile oils can also be squeezed out of it. The lemon is then to be cut into two, squeezed, and the juice mixed with 2 teaspoonfuls of glycerine and 200 ml of honey. In the case of a coughing fit a teaspoonful of the mixture is to be taken.

D. C. Jarvis recommended comb honey against sinus trouble, nasal obstruction and hay fever. The comb should be chewed for 10–15 minutes so that all the vitamin A will be drawn from it. In cases of exhaustion, twitching and tremor a spoonful of honey is to be taken after meals.

Honey also helps the functioning of the liver, it is an excellent glycogenetic. Glycogen constitutes an immediately available reserve of energy which accumulates in the liver and counteracts the accumulating fat which results in excess weight.

In his book about honey and milk powder, Walter Spöttel enumerates several physicians who, in cases of mild diabetes or a predisposition to it, suggested honey consumption to help the metabolism and stimulate the secretion of insulin.

Zaiss applied honey with success in cases of hyperacidity. Let us refer at this point to individual sensitivity again. Many people experience an unpleasant heartburn after honey consumption. This is why, in the case of any complaint, honey should only be taken after consulting one's doctor.

The detoxicating effect of honey is also important. It is especially good at mitigating the effects of morphine, chloroform and potassium cyanide, as the toxic materials may form chemical bonds with the derivatives of dextrose e.g. gluconic acid. Substantial amounts of honey may improve the condition of a patient even after snake bite or mushroom poisoning.

In addition, honey pollen is also a useful supplementary food for convalescents. It will help strengthen the patient and increase his weight. In a children's hospital near Paris the haemoglobin content of the blood of the young patients increased as a result of pollen intake, and the period of their convalescence shortened.

At the 1975 world congress of apiarists in Madrid one of the reports discussed the success

Lady with flowers and a basket. Made of strips of copper and mounted on hardwood. Déri Museum, Debrecen

ful application of pollen as part of a cure for alcoholism. It is also very good for patients undergoing psychotherapy.

Preparations containing royal jelly are sold in several countries under various fancy names, e.g. "Super Strength Royal Jelly" in the USA, "Longivex" in Canada, "Apifortyl" in the FRG and "Apiserum" in France.

The favourable effect of bee stings on arthritis is universally known. In Hungary there were also doctors who cured their patients with bee poison, sometimes actually having them stung by bees. The Lithuanian pharmaceutical factory, Sanitos, produces a preparation containing bee poison, under the name "Apitrit", and the Mack company in the FRG has one on the market which is called "Forapin R. Liniment".

Propolis was recommended as long ago as in ancient times, by Varro, to be applied in plasters on wounds. It was then forgotten for a long time. Experiments for defining its active ingredients have recently commenced in pharmaceutical factories in Hungary. In the USSR alcoholic solutions of propolis in rations of 1:10 and 3:10 are available, but in Japan, Norway and Denmark, preparations containing propolis among their ingredients are on the shelves of drugstores. They are mainly used for healing wounds.

The special effects of honey collected from different flowers

The information about the effect of honey on health and on diseases is true in general but, as with the special properties of medicinal herbs, the best results can be achieved by using a particular type of honey, from a single plant or flower. In many cases the same result is not achieved when using an infusion or extract of the same herb, as the materials accumulating in the root, stem, leaves or flower of the plant are not the same and the nectar does not contain all of them.

To illustrate what we mean we have chosen a few varieties of common honey and examined their special effects.

Acacia honey contains glucosides and volatile oils which, together with vitamins and sugars, relieves coughs and also has a disinfecting effect.

In linden-blossom honey there is, among other things, pharnesol, one of the sources of its characteristic smell. It has sedative and disinfecting effects, and it is used as a tranquilizer and anticonvulsive as well as against coughs and bronchitis. The nectar of linden blossoms, just like that of the marsh marigold, also contains choline which is particularly useful against arteriosclerosis.

Mint honey, should it come from cultivated or wild flowers has, as a result of its volatile oil content, an anaesthetic effect, it inhibits distension and, in cases of cardiospasm, biliary colic, gastric spasm and intestinal colic can be used as an anticonvulsive. Mixed flower honey containing melilot honey has similar sedative and anticonvulsive effects.

The flavonoids, volatile oils, phenol- and resin-like materials which are present in foxtail clover honey, are good for diuresis, against diarrhoea and as an expectorant.

The honey from cabbage flowers is recommended, on account of its dehydrating effect, for people on a diet and in the case of disturbances in the fluid balance.

Buckwheat honey is applied in cases of indigestion and metabolic disturbances.

Alfalfa honey is given to babies at the time of the changeover from milk to semi-solid food.

Honey from fruit-trees blossoming early in

Babe in swaddling clothes. Carved pear mould for honeycakes with the inscription *"Ladi Krausz"*, from 1812. Déri Museum, Debrecen

the spring has a high level of vitamins and minerals, whereas honey from apple blossom has a beneficial effect on the heart muscles.

The honeydew honey yielded by conifers will cleanse the respiratory tract and calm tense nerves.

Chestnut honey is useful for genital inflammations and is also considered an aphrodisiac.

The production, extraction and sale of honey made from a single kind of flower is rather demanding and costly. Its value, however, is higher than that of mixed honey as it better meets the demands of consumers and its health-protecting qualities are more pronounced.

The demand for natural food is on the increase, not only because of the side effects of medicines made of chemicals but also because the various types of honey with their different tastes, colours and consistencies are delicacies.

The booth of a Debrecen honeycake maker round the turn of the century at the Hortobágy Fair. Horse-herds in long embroidered felt cloaks and with ornamental long whips. Déri Museum, Debrecen

Honeycake-making and Related Industries

"... not far away we caught sight of a honeycake maker's booth. This was again a place to drop in. There would be an abundance of things to make gifts of. Honeycake-making is the wittiest craft. Its patron is not Mercury but Cupid. All true love, all teasing. Honeycake makers are not craftsmen actually, they are poets. With their cakes they create a cheery atmosphere, bring smiles to lips and cause cheeks to blush. You could say they spoonfeed the reader, supply him with ideas about how to philander, how to be naughty with the wenches. There is the honeycake "heart"—a gentle hint; a babe in swaddling clothes or just a cradle: a little sauciness; a horseman studded with almonds—a bit of fortune telling. But when bought by a father all figures are just pieces of sweatmeat."

Kálmán Mikszáth:★ The Black Town

After reading the poetic account of Kálmán Mikszáth let us see what a honeycake actually is.

According to the Encyclopaedia published in 1765 by Diderot and D'Alembert, the French philosophers, it is a "... honey-bread made with rye-flour. Before the honey is mixed with the flour it is boiled thoroughly for a long time, skimmed well, and while still warm, poured over the rye-flour. It is then placed in a vat, and the honey and flour are mixed with a pole." More detailed is another French description from a book by G. Kiger. "Honeycake is a brown kind of pastry made of rye-

★ (1849–1918) Hungarian novelist.

flour and honey with spices. Candied pieces of fruit, angelica, figs, dates, damsons, cherries, morello-cherries or apricots can often be found in it sometimes for decoration and in other cases to improve the taste. The most famous honeycakes in France are made in Dijon, but they are also made in the town of Rheims and in the vicinity of Paris." The French call this honeycake cum spiced milk loaf "pain d'épice" while the British, following their example, call it gingerbread, but the word ginger stands here as a synonym for every other spice as well. In Germany its name is "Honigkuchen", but they also have "Lebkuchen" which, although similar to honeycake, does not in most cases contain honey.

The Hungarian Standard makes a distinction between cake made from honey and others of a honeylike character, which "... are made of flour and honey, starch syrup, invert sugar or saccharose (cane sugar), flavouring, colouring and other additives which soften the dough after thoroughly mixing and kneading the ingredients and leaving the dough to rest. The dough is then rolled, moulded (cut into various shapes), baked and coated." Honeycakes must contain 20% honey, and cakes of a honeycake-like character 5%. Honeycake is different from any other kind. Unlike bread, it is very sweet and is not leavened but is made to rise using baking powder, salt volatile, bicarbonate of soda or pearl-ash. It is not similar to other cakes which last a long time either. They are characterized by a high cane sugar content whereas in honeycake easily digested fructose and dextrose are used. Honey by itself, or mixed with invert sugar, starch syrup or condensed must, ensures the honeycake's softness. Another advantage of honeycake over other cakes and pastries is that it keeps well.

The Germans made use of the fact that honeycakes keep well centuries ago, giving soldiers

A young woman in Hungarian gala-dress and a hussar. Carved honeycake mould. Déri Museum, Debrecen

and travellers some honeycake for the road. The French used it during the Second World War. Every month they sent five hundred tons of honeycakes to the soldiers who had been taken prisoners of war by the Germans, to improve their diet.

The history of honeycake-making

The basic activity of a honeycake maker was to separate the wax and honey from the honeycombs produced in the skeps. The honey and wax extracted in this way were his most important ingredients. From the honey, honeycake, honey-drink, honey-candies, etc. and various other pastries were made. Candles, floor-polish and several technical wax products were made from the beeswax. Bleaching the raw, yellow wax was also one of his jobs.

The predecessor of all pastries is the griddle-cake. A thick dough, made from water, flour and milk, and later, honey. It was smeared on a stone and heated by the sun until it got dry, and then it lasted for a long time.

There are archaeological findings which suggest baking took place dating back to as early as the 3rd millennia B.C. In the valley of the River Indus, a round oven and several cake moulds of stone and clay were unearthed during the Mohenjo-Daro excavations of 1933. The spiral-shaped mould found there, was also known in Egypt—it may have been a representation of the sun.

In Mesopotamia in 3000 B.C. the Sumerians had patterned cylindrical rollers to mark their clay tablets with. It is assumed that they also shaped pastry in the same way.

During the excavations of Mari, a town which used to lie on the River Euphrates some time early in the second millennia B.C. a bakery was found in one of the three hundred rooms of the palace with a round oven and forty-seven moulds, some of them still intact. It is thought that the baking traditions of the Indus Valley and Mesopotamia were interrelated.

In Egypt, between 2880 and 2860 B.C. a kind of square oven was already known. After pre-heating it the baker swept out the ash and used the grate for baking. Griddle-cakes were also stuck to the outer side of the ovens and even to the sunscorched outer walls of adobe houses. In the tomb of Ramose and Hat Nufer, who were buried in 1500 B.C., remains of man-shaped cakes, made with dates and grapes, were found in the course of the excavations made in 1936.

There are also pastry moulds dating back to the rule of Ramses III (1168–66 B.C.).

According to the Bible, Melchisedec, a Jewish priest, made excellent honeycakes more than 2000 years B.C.

The Greeks copied the idea of using moulds from the Egyptians. Four moulds dating from the fourth century B.C. are kept in a museum in Philadelphia (Pa.). It was noted of Pythagoras that he never sacrificed living animals to the gods but offered honeycakes in the shape of animals. Greek sailors took honeycakes as an offering to the temple of the god of the winds, whose goodwill was most important to them.

Honeycake gets more than a passing mention in ancient literature. In "The Clouds" by Aristophanes, honeycake is suggested as a propitiatory sacrifice to the deities, whereas in *Lysistrata* it is used as a sop to Cerberus. In his play entitled "The Knights", a prize made of honeycake is awarded to the man who can hold his liquor the best.

In Rome, the first confectioneries opened in 171 B.C. Cato, the Elder, gives a list of the sweets which could be bought there. The *forum cupedinis,* the market of gourmets, had an important role to play in the life of the town. It was there that the delicacies of honeycake makers were on sale. Martial, Pliny and Varro, describing feasts in the imperial period, mention that on the second serving table comb-honey, honeycakes and various fruits preserved in honey had an important place among the delicacies. At the Lucullian banquets they ate root vegetables, radishes and sauerkraut with honey. As a medicine, garlic was often taken with honey.

In his novel the *Golden Ass,* Apuleius (125–180 A.D.) wrote of Cerberus the dog, that it should be given a honeycake to quiet him.

In gastronomic literature, references are made even today to Apicius's cookery book written 300 B.C. which contains various meals prepared with honey.

And now a few recipes by Roman authors.

Liba sigillariata: this was a stamp-shaped cake similar to the Debrecen honeycakes made today in Hungary. (In those days it was, of course made by pressing the dough into an earthenware mould.) 450 g–16 oz. honey and 550 g–1 lb. 2 oz. flour were kneaded together. After adding a spoonful of lemon juice and some pearl-ash dissolved in water, it was kneaded again and then left to rest for a day. The next day it was rolled on a smooth table sprinkled with flour, cut into shapes, pressed into moulds, deftly taken out of the moulds and put into the oven and baked.

Eucitus or *globus* was the name of the crispy honey doughnut which was a favourite with every gourmet of the Eternal City.

We learn from Virgil that *libum* or *liba* was the name of the sacrificial honeycake which was made of wheat flour, sometimes with oil, eggs or butter and natural honey.

According to Voltier and Roger, French honeycake makers, *placentia* was the name of one of the earliest Roman pastries prepared with honey.

For the recipe of the *savillum* we are indebted to Cato himself. Flour was mixed with honey, hazelnuts and raisins and then baked in large pieces.

The *scribitta* was a small flat cake, shaped in an earthenware mould and contained more or less the same ingredients as the *liba sigillariata.*

Judging from its name, the *spira* must have been a honeycake twisted into a spiral before being baked, so that it looked like a snail's shell.

In Roman pastries there were several fine flavourings, like spices, almonds and dried grapes. We know of a recipe where the addition of leaven is recommended and probably the methods of lightening the dough with whisked egg whites or baking powder were not unknown either.

Martial wrote in one of his epigrams:

"A thousand toothsome shapes of handiwork that hand will construct for you; for him alone labours the frugal bee."*

In Ostia, the port of Rome, four hundred pastry moulds were unearthed. They date back to around 200 A. D.

Gallic legions were stationed in Aquincum, capital of the Roman Province Pannonia which used to lie on the territory of today's Óbuda, a district of Budapest, according to the evidence of the sarcophaguses now exhibited in the open air museum there. In the course of the excavations grey and red earthenware moulds were found representing Mauritius riding a ram, Pan drunk in the company of a goat, the triumphal march of Marcus Aurelius, with Marcus Aurelius himself on the back of a galloping horse, Victoria with a laurel wreath, and the

* Martial Epigrams with an English translation by Walter C. A. Ker, M. A. The Loeb Classical Library, Cambridge, Mass. Harvard University Press, London, William Heinemann Ltd. Revised edition 1968. Vol. 2. p. 517.

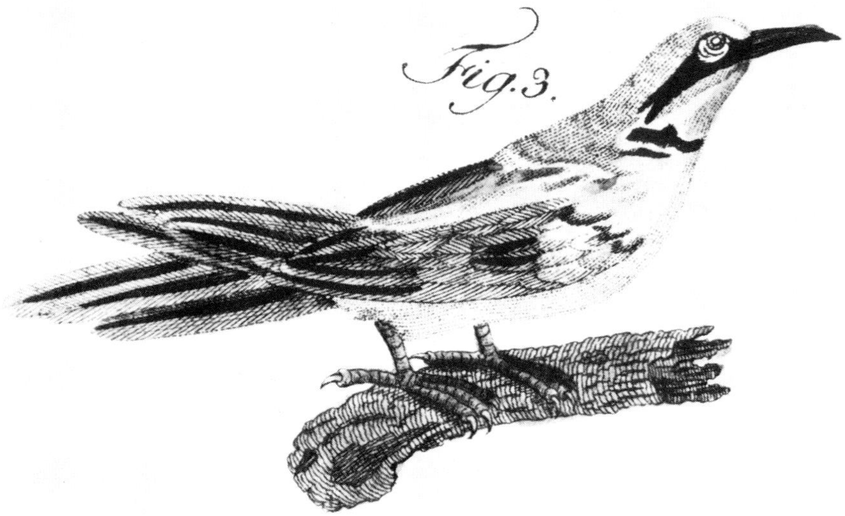

Old print representing a bee-eater (Perops apiaster) which mainly feeds on bees and wasps

hand-shake of Marcus Aurelius and Lucius Verus co-regents. These artistically elaborated moulds were used for making honeycakes, which shows that in the first centuries A.D. in the Province of Pannonia, bee-keeping was practised on a high level. The Pannonians presumably passed their knowledge on to their successors, the Celts and Germans, and they in turn to the Avars and Slavs. When the Hungarians appeared in the Carpathian Basin at the end of the ninth century, they continued the tradition.

The Vikings took dry griddle cakes along when embarking on their long sea voyages since they kept well and it was easy to soften them with water.

The Scandinavians and Germans celebrated the winter solstice. When they saw that the days were no longer getting shorter they baked a wild hog-shaped "Honigbrod" to offer as a sacrifice instead of a living animal. Later they also offered round honeycakes representing the Sun, to Odin, their Sun-god. Odin himself was also represented, in most cases riding a galloping horse. Was this perhaps the archetype of gingerbread hussars?

When celebrating Christmas, Christians also celebrated winter solstice, the renewal of life. Only now the ancient shapes were replaced by the star and the heart, the symbols of the star over the stable in Betlehem and of Christian love.

In the monastery of Tegernsee in Bavaria spicy honeycakes including one called *Pfefferzeltum* were baked, as early as the eleventh century.

In the thirteenth–fourteenth centuries honeycake makers' shops appeared one after the other in Paris, Rheims, Nuremberg, Vienna, Augsburg and several other towns. Most of them followed the tradition of some monastery.

The English "hot cross bun" baked on Good Friday has its origins in heathendom. Gingerbread in the shape of a saint or other religious symbol was an important item at the fairs organized on the occasion of a religious festival. The figures were often gilded as the merchandise had to be attractive. The ginger and other spices had made it expensive anyway, so a little gold foil did not matter too much. This is where the proverb "taking the gilt off the gingerbread" comes from.

Another sign of the importance of honeycake was that around 1200 an abbot named Bernleri, forbade monks living in monasteries from making honeycake because "every man of good sense will admit that the spices put into them are too exciting for monks and, if they season their honeycake abundantly they will find every wine sour and will pull angry faces when drinking". To appreciate the arguments of the late abbot we have to know that in those days roasts were not garnished as they are today but accompanied by piquant sauce, a mixture of must, vinegar, spices and herbs and a special honeycake made with raw grated root vegetables. Such honeycakes for grating were ordered from Hungarian honeycake makers by British buyers as late as between the two world wars. Honeycake for grating was in use in Hungary, especially in orthodox Jewish households, up to about the 1930s. It was cheap as it was made of the leftover honey washed out of the combs produced in skeps.

French honeycakes had very distinguished advocates, like the mistress of King Charles VII, Agnes Sorel, and the sister of King Francis I, Margaret of Navarre, authoress of the Heptameron.

The knowledge of Italian honeycake makers had aided the development of the French industry until Transalpine competitors were expelled from France because of rumours that King Henry III had fallen victim to poisoned honeycakes.

In February, 1595, Henry IV issued a privilege decreeing the honeycake makers' guild be directed by a guild-master. In 1596 four masters of the guild visited the workshops, fairs and parish feasts in and around the town of Chartres checking quality and forbidding those to trade who were not members of the guild or did not observe the rules governing weight, size, quality and price.

In the days of King Louis XIV, honeycake makers offered their ware with the following words: "Honeycake for the heart, in Senlis I saw those who had eaten of it getting healthy again, I offer it good-heartedly to everybody."

In 1655 there were twenty honeycake makers in Paris. In 1727, after some economic difficulties there were no more than six of them trading in spite of the fact that honeycake makers were included in the list of craftsmen accompanying the royal household. After that, honeycake-making brought fame mainly to Rheims and Dijon.

St. George and the dragon. Carved honeycake mould. 18th century. Museum of Arts and Crafts, Budapest

The first famous honeycake slab made in Rheims weighed 6 to 8 kilos and was made of honey and flour with baking powder. It was sold in slices and flavoured with lemon peel and aniseed. There were also smaller honeycakes flavoured with fragrant orange blossom oil (neroli oil) and decorated with tiny sugar pellets of various colours. In 1571 competition between bakers and pastry makers compelled honeycake makers to form their own guild. The guild prescribed rules for baking, and a list of duties for the six honeycake makers then operating in Rheims, and saw to it that quality specifications were observed. "An apprentice desirous of qualifying as a journeyman had to produce two masterpieces, a six-pound square and a four-pound round honeybread according to the learned recipes. The production of the "masterpiece" was supervised by the guild master and two old masters." The rules which were approved by the archbishop, were supplemented in 1614 by clauses providing that the sons of masters had to make the same indenture and produce "masterpieces" in the same way as those who had come from outside. This was the start of an unceasing struggle between those who only had professional skills and the privileged ones who belonged to a guild.

In 1692 bakers also started to bake honeybread. The honeycake makers brought a lawsuit against them and won, but debates went on for a long time afterwards as to which party was entitled to make this or that.

During a skirmish in 1774 between the inhabitants of Rheims and neighbouring Châlons-sur-Marne, people from the latter town sang a song saying "When we take them prisoner we shall feed all Rheims' honeycake eaters on honeycake only."

It was a custom to give gifts to distinguished guests visiting the town. On the occasion of his coronation King Henry IV received, among other things, a honeycake which the alderman of the town handed over to him with the following words: "We give you a honeycake, Rousselot pears and our hearts, in short the best of what we have."

King Louis XIV and King Charles X were also presented with honeycakes and wine when greeted enthusiastically in Rheims. When the bride of King Louis XV, travelled to Paris via Châlons-sur-Marne, besides being given the best products of the town, primarily textiles, she also got a honeycake from the citizens of Rheims which she thanked them for rapturously.

In 1770, Marie Antoinette was given the same ovation when passing through Rheims, and Marie Louise, Napoleon's wife, was also greeted with a honeycake in 1810.

The household of the Prince of Burgundy–Dijon was the capital of the duchy–stocked up on honeycakes regularly. One of the orders dated 1348, was for cinnamon, cloves, nutmeg, almonds, pepper, dates, hazelnuts, Lombard wine (whose ingredients have fallen into oblivion since then) and various sugars which were then used in the honeycake made for the court.

In 1570, the bakers' guild forbade its members from baking for honeycake makers. (It should be explained that bread was baked in very hot ovens and when the loaves were taken out it was customary to let a honeycake maker use the still-hot oven. Such common use of ovens occurred as late as between the two world wars in Hungary.) There was also argument between honeycake makers and bakers over the best spots in the market, as the owners of booths immediately flanking the paths could sell more of their goods. One of the lawsuits we know of took place in front of the Inner City Parish Church of Pest in the 1830s between a baker, János Ludvig, and a honeycake maker, Imre Beliczay.

In 1775, the pastry makers of Dijon left the honeycake makers' guild. We know the name of four Dijon honeycake makers operating in 1777 and that in 1780 their guild had ten members. Honeycake makers had very plain shops in those days: a small room next to the workshop with a door opening to the street. (There was a famous little shop of this type in Attila Street, Budapest years ago, owned by Samu Benedek and later by his daughter.)

In 1938 there were 14 honeycake makers employing 40 to 50 assistants each, and 4 with about 200 employees in Dijon.

The first mention made of honeycake makers in Nuremberg was in 1108. In 1276 they were in the same guild as the bakers who ridiculed them for their various puny little pastries. It was recorded that the soldiers of Hildesheim were, in addition to their regular rations, given honeycakes from the time when Hildesheim joined the Hanseatic League in the thirteenth century.

It was customary for nuns to present their

relatives with honeycakes for New Year's Day. Margarete Emser, a nun, sent some needlework, a candle and a honeycake to Master Heinrich who lived in Nördling.

As early as 1368 two Viennese honeycake makers were mentioned by name.

We know of honeycake makers working in Schweidnitz (Silesia) in 1293, in Basle, at about the same time and in Frankfurt in 1326. Heinrich, a honeycake maker, is mentioned in the records of Ulm in 1350, and Uli Pabstel in those of Munich in 1370.

In 1393 the Basle "Herrenzunft von Safran" had 34 members. Only honeycake makers who had paid their membership dues to the guild were allowed to sell their goods at fairs. In the course of a lawsuit conducted in Vienna in 1394, mention was made of Ewenhardt, a honeycake maker from Regensburg. Between 1413 and 1453 several honeycake makers worked, according to tradition, in the same street, the Weidengasse in Vienna. They were "Anna die Lebzelterin, Jakob Dürr der Lebzelter" and other "servants of the honeycake industry".

It was in those times that the first carved honeycake moulds, representing events from Jesus' life appeared, like the "Passio domini nostri Jesu Christi". Some people suppose the origins of the word *Lebkuchen* to come from the phrase *"Kuchen des Lebens"*–pastry of life, or pastry representing life.

On the occasion of the 1431 Council of Basle, honeycakes were distributed among the people. This then became a widespread habit. When Emperor Frederick III of Austria attended the Nuremberg Diet in 1487 and saw the enormous number of children playing in the wide moat, he had honeycakes bearing his own effigy made and distributed among them. Later it often happened that honeycakes were distributed with the portrait of the ruling monarch on them.

When the Marquis of Brandenburg visited Nuremberg with his wife in 1496, he was welcomed with gifts by the distinguished honeycake makers of the town.

The first independent honeycake makers' guild was formed in 1530 in Nuremberg to give efficient protection to its members against the competition of bakers, pretzel- and pastrymakers on the market.

Kurze
Anleitung
für das
Landvolk,
in Absicht
auf die Bienen-Wirthschaft,
wie solche mit Nutzen geführet
werden soll.
Für die Kais. Königl. Erbländer,
insonderheit aber für das
Königreich Hungarn
eingerichtet.
Worinnen deutlich gezeiget wird, wie durch
eine wohl eingerichtete Bienen-Wirthschaft in
kurzer Zeit ein beträchtliches Vermögen ge-
sammlet werden könne.
Alles aus eigener Erfahrung zusammen
getragen, und zum Nutzen des Landmannes in
Fragen und Antworten eingerichtet.
Nebst
einem kleinen Bienen-Kalender
für die Bienen Väter,
und mit nützlichen Kupfern gezieret.
Preßburg und Leipzig,
auf Kosten der neuen Buchhandlung Anton Löwens,
1773.

"Kurze Anleitung für das Landvolk, in Absicht auf die Bienen-Wirtschaft... insonderheit aber für das Königreich Ungarn eingerichtet." Pozsony, and Leipzig, 1773. Title-page

The Forest of Spessart lies not far from Frankfurt. It was in this region that the Grimm brothers collected the tale of Hansel and Gretel with the gingerbread house and the witch. Hansel and Gretel were the children of a poor woodcutter. At the time of the peasant insurrections poverty was so abject that the parents decided to take the children to the woods and leave them to their fate. Everyone knows this story. A teacher named Hans Traxler studied the scene very thoroughly and published a book in 1978, under the title *Die Wahrheit über Hänsel und Gretel*. He says that he found the house of the woodcutter, the glade between the two clearings where the children were "allegedly" led by their father, the oven and the tools, even the recipes hidden between the rocks. Continuing his research he learned in Wernigerode of a woman honeycake maker, Katharina Schrader, who had been courted by a certain Hans Metzler. One night in 1647 Katharina Schrader fled Wernigerode and bought a house in Spessart forest where she set up honeycake making facilities. She invented and made all kinds of honeycakes for sale at fairs, to monasteries and houses of the gentry. She invented filled honeycakes, made Merseburg Nutmeg Honeycakes, candied ones—using the Bamberg method, syrupy honeycakes and Gelnhausen "Leckerli". Business was so good that competitors became envious of her. Metzler denounced her to the Gelnhausen municipal court as a witch. According to the records of the case she rode a broomstick, lured people into her house where she confined, fattened and then ate them. We know what terrible consequences were ensued from the charge of being a witch in those days. Katharina denied the charges even when tortured with the thumbscrew. She knew that if she was declared a witch she would be burnt at the stake. In the end the accusation was dropped.

Hans Metzler, however, could not reconcile himself to the judgement. With his sister, Gretel, he went to the forest, found Katharina's house, broke in, killed her, and pushed her into one of the hot ovens. Metzler, who was honeycake purveyor by appointment in Nuremberg, continued to make his honeycakes unpunished. In Traxler's book, which appeared in Frankfurt in 1978, there are photos of the objects and documents used as proof, including the cover of the records of the 1651 witchcraft trial.

In 1697 the town council of Nuremberg decreed a design patent. Every honeycake maker was only allowed to use his own carved moulds and was forbidden to make ones even similar those of others. It was decreed at the same time that *Magenbrot,* which was to keep the digestion in order, and *Saucekuchen* for grinding, could only be made by honeycake makers. It was also announced that every honeycake maker must have his own oven: *Jeder Lebzelter soll seinen eigenen Rauch haben*.

In the days of Frederick the Great, King of Prussia, it happened that Subis, an Austrian general fell in love with a girl in Leipzig. Gabriel Bergfried, a honeycake maker, had already serious intentions towards her. The adventuresome general seized countless valuables, including honeycakes in Leipzig, expecting that he would return victorious and take everything with him including the girl. However, he lost the Battle of Rohrbach and had to flee. He left everything behind including the large parcel of square honeycakes wrapped in shining paper. Bergfried put labels on them showing a picture of the general on horseback on the run. He named the honeycake *Subischen* and earned a lot of money from it. The girl became the honeycake maker's wife and every year the couple celebrated the anniversary of the Rohrbach battle (1757).

The names of the most famous types of honeycake in Germany were *Printen* made in Aachen, *Brenten* in Frankfort, *Pfeffernüsse* in

Offenbach, *Honigkuchen* in Vienna, *Leckrli* in Basle and in Poland, and *Kathrinchen* in Torun.

Honeycake makers had their hey-day in the fifteenth–eighteenth centuries. Their role was later taken over by confectioners and large-scale industrial plants. In Poland more richly decorated types of honeycake became usual after the Renaissance.

In Russian territories they make *kholobki* and *hvorost* and in the Ukraine, polianitzi, knishy and bihantzi were made. Their collective name is *prianik*=honeycake. The honeycakes made in Suzdal are still famous.

The history of making cakes and drinks from honey in Hungary

At the time of the Arpadian kings, monasteries had their own apiaries making their own wax candles for the church, wax figures as votive offerings; they also made honeycakes and honey drinks.

Monks were assisted by a remarkable number of peasants and craftsmen. Later, small settlements were formed around the monasteries by the craftsmen and their children who were given to the monastery by royal patent. During the reign of King Matthias Corvinus there were honeycake makers who used oriental spices imported via Vienna.

From the accounts of Besztercebánya (today Banska Bystrica, Czechoslovakia) it has come to light that in 1382 more than one honeycake maker was granted civic rights in the town.

There was a honeycake maker operating in Pozsony in 1440, and not long after, another in Sopron. The development of the honeycake industry soon started in Transylvania too, where Brassó and Nagyszeben were the centres which sent honey, wax and honeycakes not only to

Portrait of Matthias II, made on the occasion of his coronation as King of Hungary. Carved honeycake mould. Walnut, 1608. Museum of Arts and Crafts, Budapest

neighbouring settlements, but also to Constantinople, Vienna and even Venice.

"Tordai pogátsa", a honeycake whose shape recalled heathen traditions (according to some people it was a fertility symbol) became famous within a short time. An almost round honeycake was stuck to each corner of the practically square piece of dough, then it was brushed with beaten egg yolk and its top cut lengthwise so that it opened up in the course of baking. It was made by heating 300 g–11 oz. honey and 200 g–7 oz. sugar with 200 ml–⅓ pint milk, to 114 °C (this is the "long-thread" stage, i.e. after taking a sample by dipping the stirring spoon into the mixture a long thread can be pulled with two fingers from it). After cooling, 600 g–1¼ lb. wheat flour was added, mixed well with the other ingredients and the dough set aside to rest for two days. After that, one egg was added, 100 g–4 oz. butter, 20 g–1 oz. salt volatile, ½ g–2/7 dram each of finely ground cinnamon, cloves and allspice, then a pinch of black pepper. This was then kneaded thoroughly. After shaping and brushing the 30–40 g–1¼–1½ oz. pieces with egg yolk, they were baked in a medium oven. Some honeycake makers boiled a sugar syrup until a short thread could be pulled from it with their fingers, mixed it with whipped egg whites, and covered the freshly baked cakes with the mixture. The honeycakes were then put back into the oven and dried.

From an inventory of his estate we can learn what kind of equipment was taken along by a honeycake maker in the eighteenth century when he set off on his journey to a fair or parish feast. The large quantity of goods taken can be gauged from the written pleading of a lawsuit conducted in Kassa in 1725. A master sued his journeyman, to whom he had handed over 82 thousand pieces of honeycake for sale at a fair, and who could only account for 55 thousand pieces.

Even as late as the sixteenth and seventeenth centuries most honeycake makers in Transdanubia paid their member's subscription, the so-called *Jahresschillinge* to the Vienna guild. The Pozsony guild received its imperial privilege in 1681. Honeycake makers' guilds were formed on the basis of royal privilege: in 1724 in Besztercebánya, in 1727 in Kassa, in 1735 in Lőcse (today Levoča, Czechoslovakia), Késmárk (today Kežmarok, Czechoslovakia) and Eperjes (today Prešov, Czechoslovakia). At the same time after a break of slightly less than a century, they were formed in 1824 in Pécs and in 1832 in Újvidék (today Novi Sad, Yugoslavia). The honeycake makers of Pest only received permission to found a guild in 1834.

In olden times many honeycake makers came to Hungary from abroad. It is assumed that some of the honeycake makers and candle-dippers (*cerearii* and *pistardii*) working here under the Arpadian kings were also of foreign origin.

Honeycakes had already been made for a long time in Debrecen when the masters were granted a charter by the town, enabling them to form their own guild in 1713. Their right was confirmed by King Charles III in 1726. The last clause of the patent confirms the condition of earlier times stating that if masters did not observe the regulations they would revert to the pre-1713 legal insecurity.

As a matter of interest it should be mentioned that in Karcag, Kézdivásárhely (today Tîrgu Secuiesc, Rumania) and Marosvásárhely (today Tîrgu Mureş, Rumania) making honeycake was mainly a woman's pursuit. It was also the women who took their very interesting ware to market—those made in Karcag being particularly intricate.

For making honeycakes several kinds of moulds were needed. From the fifteenth century moulds were carved from wood. The idea of carving may have come to Hungary from the southern parts of Germany and Poland.

The collection of carved honeycake moulds kept in the Budapest Museum of Arts and Crafts is famous. It was started by Ágoston Szalai in the nineteenth century. As well as carvings on religious subjects (The Adoration of the Magi, Madonna with Child, Christ on the Cross, etc.) or representing scenes from Greek–Roman mythology, there are many portraits of rulers (Gustavus Adolphus of Sweden, Ferdinand III and IV, Leopold II, Matthias II, Mihály Apafi). A full figure of Lajos Kossuth was carved on a honeycake mould.

Well known Hungarian mould-carvers included Georg Sonntag in 1721, Paulus Czechmeister, a Győr honeycake maker in 1797 who marked his carvings with the initials PZ and CZ,

András Szép, a mould-carver and honeycake maker in Somogy county, and Imre Beliczay, who was born in 1806 and used the initials EP and BI. The firm founded by Zechmeister was still in existence in the nineteenth century and his son became mayor of the town of Győr. Leander Zitterbarth who was also a honeycake maker, marked his products with the initials ZL. One of the last honeycake makers who carved his own moulds was Sándor Szikszai who

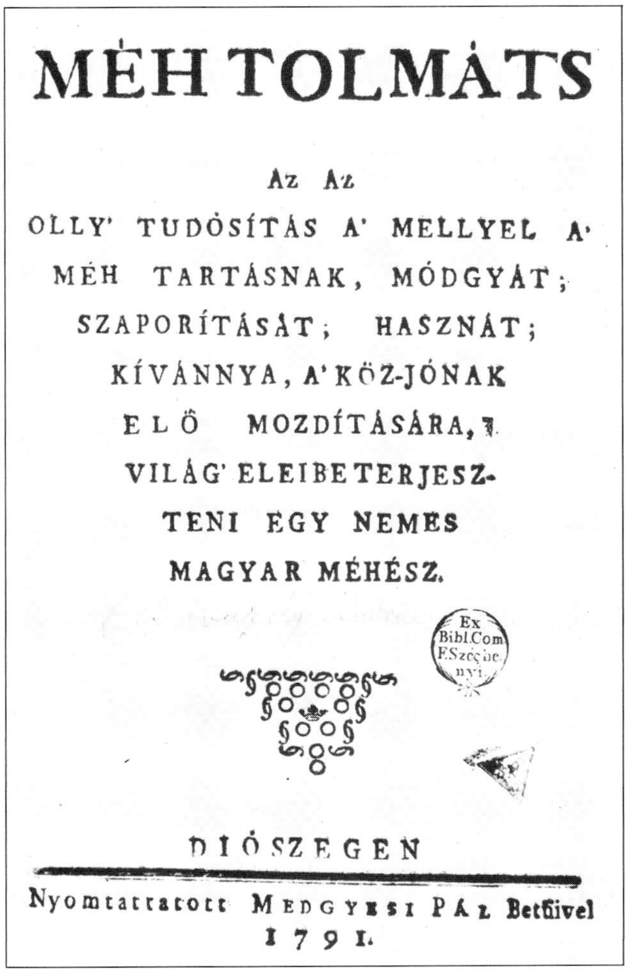
MÉH TOLMÁTS

Az Az

OLLY' TUDÓSÍTÁS A' MELLYEL A' MÉH TARTÁSNAK, MÓDGYÁT; SZAPORÍTÁSÁT; HASZNÁT; KÍVÁNNYA, A' KÖZ-JÓNAK ELŐ MOZDÍTÁSÁRA, 's VILÁG' ELEIBE TERJESZTENI EGY NEMES MAGYAR MÉHÉSZ.

DIÓSZEGEN

Nyomtattatott MEDGYESI PÁL Betűivel 1791.

András Ravaszdi: *Méh tolmáts* (Bee Interpreter), the book of "a noble Hungarian bee-keeper". Diószeg, 1791

worked until as late as the beginning of the twentieth century. His figures included a locomotive and a bicycle.

The most beautiful moulds date back to the seventeenth and eighteenth centuries. Not only because in those days goldsmiths and other craftsmen better versed in the arts carved some moulds, but also because much more time was devoted to the preparation of a mould.

In the second half of the nineteenth century artistic honeycakes in relief were replaced by market wares, the red heart, the hussar, the doll and the slippers.

Several craftsmen who had come from abroad soon became filled with local patriotism for Hungary. The Pest honeycake makers' guild issued certificates of mastership in Hungarian as soon as 1834.

The Hungarian honeycake industry thrived up to the beginning of the nineteenth century after which the start of beet sugar making and the invention of stearin restricted it. This is neatly set out in the analysis submitted by Imre Beliczay, guild master in chief of the Pest honeycake makers' guild to the Országos Iparegyesület (National Industrial Association) in 1843, registered under No. 11 on the 2nd of September. (Manuscript in the possession of Dr. László Beliczay's family.)

"As I mentioned in my note to the esteemed Industrial Association dated the 19th August, Pest, the rest of what I have to say, I will present later, if I do not inconvenience the esteemed Industrial Association ... There is not a branch of agriculture more profitable than bee-rearing or which outstrips any produce in respect of profitability. Let us presume, for example, that the population of a village has 100 or even 1000 skeps of honey. They would not need larger fields, pastures, forests, etc. because everyone knows that bees collect their treasure from flowers. Nowhere in the world can agriculture pro-

Quod erga humillimam Fidelium Nostrorum CIVIUM & MAGISTRORUM CEROPLASTARUM in Libera Regiaq. CIVITATE Nostra PESTIENSI degentium & commorantium Supplicationem MAJESTATI Nostræ in eo factam, quatenus NOS Eosdem, pro meliori inter Ipsos servando Ordine, certis Articulis CAEHALIBUS, in conformitate benigne stabilitorum per NOS Generalium Principiorum clementer providere, talesq. ARTICULOS, omniaque & singula in iisdem contenta, ratos, gratos & accepta habentes, Literis Nostris Privilegialibus inseri & inscribi facientes, authoritate Nostra Cæsareo Regia approbare, roborare, ratificare, ac pro mentionatis Civibus & Magistris CEROPLASTIS, Ipsorumq. Successoribus Universis valituros, benigne confirmare dignaremur. Quorum quidem Articulorũ germanico Idiomate conscriptor. Tenor talis est.

Erster Artikel.
Von den Lehrjungen.

Derjenige, welcher als Lehrjung aufgenommen zu werden wünscht, kann was immer für einer gesetzlich angenommenen Religion seyn. Wenn ein Lehrjung mit Vorwissen und Zustimmung seiner Vorstehers, und zwar bey Gelegenheit der vierteljährigen Zunfthaltung, gehörig aufgenommen, und in die Lehre eingeschrieben wird, muss selber bey seinem Meister, bey welchem er in die Lehre einzutreten

DATUM

per manus Fidelis Nostri Nobis sincere Dilecti Spectabilis ac
Magnifici Comitis ADAMI REVICZKY de Revisnye
Insignium Ordinum Sti Stephani Regis Aplici Magnae Crucis,
Leopoldi vero Imperatoris [illegible] Sti Mau-
ritii & Lazari magnae Crucis in adamantibus Equitis, Camera-
rii, & actualis Intimi Status Consiliarii Nostri, Curiae Nrae Regiae
per Hungariam Magistri, Cottus Borsodiensis Supremi Comitis
nec non per Regnum Hgriae Aulae Nostrae prout et Ins. Ordinis
Sti Stephani R. Aplici Cancellarii, in Imper. Urbe Nra Vienna
Austriae, die trigesima M. Januarii, Anno Dni Millesimo Octingentesimo
trigesimo quarto, Regnor. Nror. Hgriae, Bohemiae, & reliquor. quadragesimo
secundo.

Franciscus

Comes Adamus Reviczky

Antonius Hadáry

Privilegium Senatui ... Civibus & ... Ceroplastis in L. Reg. Civit. Pestien. ...

The charter of incorporation of the Pest honeycake makers' and candle-dippers' guild dated 1834 and signed by Emperor Franz

duce wealth from more or less nothing, and yet regrettably it is still neglected. What can we do about it? The solution to this question and acting upon it would bring millions to our beloved country. However, I am not saying every region is suitable for bee-keeping, I only mean that there are parts of which we know for sure.

"Honey and wax can always be sold at a good price. I say a good price, because even if a quintal of honey could fetch 6 pengős and a quintal of wax 40 forints it would still be a good price. However, this is not the case since honey costs 13–16 forints, and the price of yellow wax is 82–86, sometimes even 92 forints, and there is always a ready market for them, though these days less at home than abroad. Potato honey, which is much less profitable, and sugar, have spoilt the market for the former, and stearin for the latter. I cannot cease to marvel at the economic system, when I hear that they chemically want to extract sweetness from any plant containing it, by any means possible though all these plants together cannot approach honey either in respect of its sweetness or healthiness —not even sugar; whereas bee-keeping, which could result in greater success, is given very little attention..."

Of the sales of Imre Beliczay master honeycake maker, we know that in 1842 he exported 80–100 quintals (8–10 metric tons) of yellow wax and 50–60 quintals (5–6 metric tones) of beeswax to Odessa and Moravia, which he had bleached himself and delivered to Upper Hungary. He made plain honeycake slabs and figures, too. Honeycake slabs were made in the following way: 100 kg – 220 lb. warm baking honey was mixed with 100 kg – 220 lb. flour and set aside to rest for three to four months. (If the master had enough capital he rested it even longer.) Before baking, "perkli" *(Bröckl)* was added to the dough, which consisted of wax, pork fat, flour and egg yolks with a little salt volatile and potash.

The Three Magi in Bethlehem.
Carved honeycake mould. Early 18th century.
Inscription: F. E. 1768. Museum of Arts and Crafts, Budapest

They also made "schiffli" for grating, substituting a thinner honey (nahsam) for pure baking honey which they mixed with the same amount of flour. This, too, was laid aside to rest for some weeks. Before baking, 25 kg – 2 quarters of granulated sugar boiled in 10 litres – 2 gallons of water and 120 egg yolks were added to the dough. One kilo of honeycake for grating was finally cut into 42 rectangular slabs.

The honeycake-making trade started to decline about one hundred years ago. In 1873 as many as 1957 honeycake makers worked in Hungary while in 1884 there were not more than 1268. Slowly they withdrew to rural areas where parish feasts and fairs ensured them a living. Gyula Fábián wrote in an article published in 1913, that the craft of honeycake making had declined and was only just existing.

An exception to the above trend was the honeycake industry of Debrecen, where uncoloured honey slabs shaped in charming wooden moulds were made as hussars, dolls and townscapes. In Debrecen, the whole procedure of baking a honeycake was called "ovening" ("kemencézés"). One of its characteristics is that honey is not boiled before being mixed with the flour, resulting in a product which retains more of the taste of the honey. The dough is then shaped using nicely carved moulds.

The ingredients of a Debrecen honeycake (adapted to household quantities) are as follows: 300 g – 11 oz. honey, 200 g – 7 oz. loaf sugar or lump sugar pounded to powder, 2 g – 1 dram salt volatile dissolved in water and 700 g–1 lb. 7 oz. wheat flour. The ingredients are mixed and then kneaded well, rolled out to a thickness of 4–8 cm–1½–3 inches depending on the depth of the mould. The dough is pressed into the floured mould and then carefully taken or knocked out. Then put 10–12 pieces on top of each other, with the shaped sides turned towards each other, and left until the dough absorbs the flour and the surface is shiny. The cakes are then put on baking sheets and into special, huge ovens with an open flame. Before baking, the embers are pushed over to the left side of the oven and the area for baking swept clean, and even wiped with a wet cloth. Two logs are then put on the embers so that the fire will have flames. The flames rise towards the chimney over the cakes and this is why the representations or patterns in relief will be a darker brown than the rest of the cake and the shapes will be more pronounced. In the course of baking, the baking sheet is pushed around within the oven in an anti-clockwise direction and the cakes take about 4 minutes to bake. Ovening was a most tiring job. Shaping was done in the morning, at noon the fire was made in the oven and baking itself started at 3 p.m. After baking, the flour was swept off the figures which were then cooled and wrapped in cellophane. There were times when they also made slabs and hearts 50 to 60 centimetres–1¾–2 feet in diameter. As there were no moulds large enough, they made them up from smaller parts. For example the large church of Debrecen was surrounded by a flower pattern and finished off with plain dough at the edges.

An important piece of furniture in the honeycake maker's workshop was the *brech* (desk) on which the dough was kneaded. This desk was 50 cm high, with a 70 by 60 cm working surface and 10 cm edges. One end was made into a seat while the other end was open. The dough was put on the top, pressed, and its thickness made even, by the lowering, raising and lowering again of a pole. The pole, which was about one

The oven of Sándor Kerékgyártó,
a Debrecen honeycake maker

and a half metres long and a little thicker than a carriage beam, was fastened to the *brech* between the legs of the seated journeyman, who adjusted the dough so it was under the pole and sprinkled the desk with flour lest the dough should stick to it. Ten to twelve kilos of dough at a time were put onto a *brech* to work with.

The master, his wife, the journeyman and the apprentice

The rules of the guilds also closely controlled human and professional relationships.

When comparing customs and journeymen's credentials in the eighteenth and nineteenth centuries in Besztercebánya (today Banská Bystrica, Czechoslovakia) and Debrecen, it can be observed that the traditions were preserved by the rules.

The certificate of mastership of Imre Beliczay honeycake maker and wax-chandler dating from 1832. Private collection

In the eighteenth century the parents or guarantors indentured the boy who wanted to be an apprentice, a disciple of the master who bound himself to initiating the child into the mysteries of the trade. Guilds restricted the number of apprentices: a master was allowed to take on one apprentice, and then, when that one had had one year of experience, another one. If the parents were serfs they had to ask for the landlord's permission for their son to learn. The time of apprenticeship was two to four years. In the first and second years the apprentice was only given pocket money. He was clad by his parents and if he caused any damage his parents were bound to pay compensation. "He burnt two baking tins of sifli—30 fillérs ... He answered back and was naughty, I sent him home," such notes can be found in the diary kept by Mrs. Károly Zechmeister about her husband's apprentices in Győr. The monthly wages of a journeyman was 2–3 forints in the middle of the nineteenth century. The re-soling of a pair of shoes (80 krajcárs) was deducted. Second-hand clothes, a coat, perhaps even a shirt was bought for him, and the prices carefully listed and also deducted from his wages. Boots and apron, however, had to be provided by the master. Only legitimate children could be employed as apprentices. The journeyman gave orders to the apprentice and if the boy repeatedly made mistakes he was entitled to slap him on the face. Nobody was allowed to employ a journeyman or itinerant journeyman without the knowledge of the guild-master. The trial period was 2 to 6 weeks for apprentices and not more than 4 weeks for journeymen.

Further rules include: The apprentice shall be disciplined, loyal and diligent, shall not incur debts as they will have to be paid either by him or by his guarantor. If an apprentice runs away during the contracted period his guarantor is bound to take him back to his master. The apprentice was allowed to turn to the guild if he experienced insults but his case was seldom upheld. He was forbidden to make friends with street urchins.

Itinerant journeymen were greeted with: "Welcome, craftsman, God has brought you along," and a handshake. When the resident journeyman was not at home, the apprentice showed him his accomodation, held the light and helped him take off his clothes.

A further 30 points detail the rules and duties of an apprentice, and only few, his rights. After the four-year apprenticeship, he was allowed to present himself for examination, and after passing the exam he was released from his apprenticeship and was acquainted with the duties and rights of journeymen. A journeyman had to do work useful to his master. The rules governing his duties covered all aspects of his life from merry-making in the evenings to the way of showing respect towards the master and his family.

A resident journeyman also had to look after the itinerant journeyman. When the latter arrived he received him with the following words: „Dear brother please tell me what your name is, where and from whom you studied," etc. Then the arrival's letter of introduction was examined, and he was asked about the greetings he had brought from his first master and from those whose workshops he had stayed in during his journey. If he gave plausible answers they took him in.

A journeyman had a fortnight's holiday. When he had spent three years with his master followed by a three-year journey, he could apply for guild membership. His application was judged on the basis of the masterpiece he had to make. This took place in the presence of two or more masters. Ingredients and tools were placed at his disposal by the master.

An apprentice and journeyman were given full board and lodging by the master, including lighting and, in most cases, laundry, too. However, they had to ask for permission if they wanted to stay out late. There were honeycake makers in Hungary on whose premises the same rules prevailed even after the Second World War, the only difference being that they gave normal wages to both apprentices and journeymen.

Souvenir card of the 1873 universal exhibition in Vienna addressed to Béla Beliczay, honeycake maker and wax-chandler. Private collection

The Organization and Operation of Apiculture in Hungary

At the present time about 40,000 people are engaged in bee-keeping in Hungary, and approximately 700,000 colonies are producing

"Húszas tányér" circular mould, carved of wood for making honeycake plates (which sold at 20 krajcárs), representing the Great Church of Debrecen, and a coat of arms. Inscription *"Kerékgyártó S. Debreczen"* Déri Museum, Debrecen

honey. There are 550 specialized groups affiliated to the General Consumers' and Produce Disposal Co-operatives. The interests of these specialized groups are protected and represented on the county level by the associations of the co-operatives, and at national level by the National Council of Consumers' Co-operatives. Work and development are coordinated by Hungaronektár, the National Centre of Apicultural Co-operatives.

Specialized groups within co-operatives contract for and purchase honey from producers. It is then forwarded to Hungaronektár which processes it in its modern plant. Honey for domestic consumption will then be handed over to wholesalers while honey for sale abroad will be exported by the Monimpex Hungarian Foreign Trading Company under the contract concluded with Hungaronektár.

Bee-keepers maintain contact with the Research Institute for the Breeding of Small Animals in Gödöllő, whose Bee-rearing Department conducts research into both bee-rearing and honey production. It also regularly studies the pollinating activity of bees and maintains contact between the large co-operative and state farms and bee-keepers, and keeps the latter informed of the latest results of research both at home and abroad.

By organizing apicultural activities in this way, we can ensure the prevention of inferior varieties of honey from being marketed, and that the quality of the honey produced totally meets the strict requirements of honey standards prevailing in Hungary and in foreign countries. As a result of permanent professional management and spot checks, the quality of honey produced for sale is stable and competitive.

Hungary wishes to increase apicultural production by establishing large-scale apiaries with three aims in view. The first is the production of larger quantities, the second, further improvement of quality, and the third, the increasing of yields through the pollinating activity of bees.

Plans for developing apiculture include the purchase of modern machinery for the central plant of Hungaronektár, the increase of processing capacity and the even higher degree of success in meeting quality requirements. The achievement of higher yields of acacia honey is also envisaged.

Supporting the work of apiaries also belongs to Hungaronektár's field of activities. They are augmenting the uniform system of hives with new types and providing trucks for transportation, further facilitating migratory bee-keeping. These special trucks are equipped with containers and motor-driven lever bars which mean a substantial decrease in human labour and consequently the speeding up of migration, and the better use of bee pastures. The export of bee colonies will also be boosted.

Not only those bee-masters who are organized into co-operatives are supported in Hungary, but also individual apiarists. Hungaronektár contracts to pay stable prices for honey which means security for producer and minimizes their risks.

Hungarian honey abroad

Hungarian acacia, linden and other varieties of honey have been known for centuries in foreign countries. It is very much sought after for its very agreeable special aroma and its reliable, fine quality. The bulk of Hungarian honey export, as has already been mentioned, is acacia honey, collected from large acacia forests. Acacia honey has the advantage that it retains its pleasant aroma for a long time and, unlike other types of honey, does not crystallize. Other honey originating from the flowers of several kinds of wild and cultivated plants (sunflower, rape, etc.) is put on the market as multiflower honey. The bulk of honey produced is sold abroad. Honey consumption in Hungary is comparatively low, not more than 300 g–11 oz. per capita annually. Hungarians have got accustomed to sugar, which is much cheaper.

Hungarian honey exports were as follows in the last thirty years:

Honey export in metric tons annually

1950/54	1962/66	1974	1981	1982
660	4485	7200	11799	13500

Hungary exported more than twenty times as much honey in 1982 as it averaged in 1950/54.

Black earthen vessel for candle dipping ornamented with "fingertip" imprint and stylized flowers from the middle of the 18th century. Déri Museum, Debrecen

This increase has been uninterrupted in recent years and is continuing. More than two thirds of Hungarian honey exports go to western European countries but there also are substantial shipments to far-away destinations.

The importance of Hungary as a honey exporter is well illustrated when we look at the export data of 1978.

Country	Metric ton
Mexico	44,959
People's Republic of China	28,120
Argentina	27,000
USA	10,144
Hungary	8,000 (13,500 in 1982)
Canada	6,701
Spain	5,100
Cuba	5,000
Bulgaria	4,348
Australia	4,274
Brazil	4,000
Federal Republic of Germany	3,801
Rumania	3,500

The following proportions of Hungarian honey exports were taken by the following major importing countries:

Country	%
FRG	21.6
UK	9.7
Sweden	7.1
Austria	16.7
France	8.1
The Netherlands	8.0
Belgium	5.2
Switzerland	1.4
Iraq	4.8
Cyprus	4.8
Other importers	12.6
Total	100.0%

The organization of bee-keeping in Hungary

In Hungary anybody can pursue the craft of bee-keeping, sit for exams and get qualifications. Courses and lectures are organized and exchanging experiences serves to further professional development.

Vocational training and extension training for adults takes place at Hungaronektár's trade school for apiarists in Zalaapáti; 2500 to 3000 people attend this school annually, participating in courses of varying length or exchanging experiences.

The most important rules of bee-hygiene are summarized in Departmental Orders which

Black earthen vessel for candle dipping with stylized flowers dating from 1819. Déri Museum, Debrecen

must be known and observed by all apiarists. Rules for spraying are regulated by the government. Conditions governing transportation of bees, methods of carrying out migration and the requirements for bee pastures are regulated by a Departmental Order. Bees can, for example, only be transported if they are covered by a veterinary certificate issued not more than thirty days in advance. This is to prevent any epidemic spreading. In the case of certain dangerous epidemics, like American foul brood and tracheal mite, the infected colonies are to be exterminated. The estimated value of the colonies destroyed on account of disease, which it is obligatory to declare, will be refunded to the bee-keepers by the state if he has acted in compliance with regulations.

Bee colonies, honey or other apicultural products, can only be exported with a permit from the Bee-rearing Department of the National Institute for Animal-hygiene.

Food and Drink Made with Honey

Bottling

Honey is particularly suitable for preserving fruit, and for making bottled fruit, jams and pastry.

Bottled fruit without steaming
Ingredients: 2-2½ kg–4–5 lb. fruit, 1 kg–2 lb. honey, 5 g–⅕ oz. salicyl.
Wash, clean and stone the fruit then put it in clean, dry jars and pour the boiling hot mixture of honey and 600 ml–1 pint water on it. Spread the salicyl evenly on top of each jarful, then cover the jars with cellophane, fasten them with a piece of string or a rubber band, then put the jars into a basket or container well lined with old newspapers or straw. Cover it well and keep it at room temperature for 24 hours. Store the jars in a larder or cool place.

Bottled steamed fruit
Ingredients: 4 kg–9 lb. fruit, 2 kg–4 lb. honey, 800 ml–1⅓ pint milk, 1 egg white.
Wash, clean and stone the fruit. Boil the honey with the milk, and mix with the whipped egg white. Strain the mixture thereby removing part of the protein which has precipitated from the milk. Pour the hot mixture on the fruit, sprinkle with a pinch of salicyl from the point of a knife and cover with cellophane. Wrap the jars in old newspapers, put them into a large pot lined with old newspapers, pour hot water and bring to the boil. Take the pot off the cooker and cover with a blanket. Leave for 24 hours, then take the jars out of the pot and keep them in a cool place.

If you wish to save money, you may prepare the syrup from 500 g–16 oz. honey and 1.25 kg–1 lb. 8 oz. of sugar.

Pear preserve

Ingredients: 2 kg–4 lb. pears, 1 kg–2 lb. honey, 600 ml–1 pint water.

Add the water to 800 g–1 lb. 11 oz. of honey

Print of a kitchen in the 19th century

and bring to the boil. Wash, peel and slice the pears then cook in the hot syrup until half-cooked. After an interval of 24 hours bring to the boil again and add 100 g–4 oz. of honey. Do the same on the third day, then put the pear slices into jars, pour over the syrup and cover with cellophane. No steaming is required.

Morello cherries for pastries and sauces
These can be preserved for use in home-made cakes and other sweets, as a decoration, flavour or a substitute for raisins or currants.
Ingredients: 5 kg–11 lb. morello cherries, 1.30 kg–2 lb. 11 oz. honey, 5 g–⅕ oz. preservative (salicyl).
Wash, clean and stone the morello cherries, put them into a large bowl, pour the honey over them and stir several times. After 24 hours put the fruit and juice into jars, sprinkle a pinch of salicyl on top and cover with cellophane. Steam the jars in a pot and when cool keep them in the larder or a cool place. Cherries can be preserved in the same way, but in this case 500 g–1 lb. more honey should be used.

Orange juice with honey
Ingredients: 2½ kg–5 lb. oranges, 1 kg–2 lb. acacia honey, 500 ml–1 pint milk, 1 egg white.
Wash the oranges and remove the zest. Squeeze the oranges and collect the juice in a china bowl. Add the pieces of thin orange peel and leave for half a day. Bring the honey and milk to the boil, mix with the whipped egg white then skim. Strain the peel off the orange juice and add the latter to the honey-and-milk mixture. If you wish to store the drink, filter it, pour it into bottles and cool it.

"Szíves húszas". A heart carved of hard wood with an Empire style vase in the middle flanked by music makers. 36x28 cm. 2nd half of the 19th century. Déri Museum, Debrecen

Baking and cooking with honey

Raspberry-squash for ice cream, pastries and drinks
Ingredients: 1.20 kg–2½ lb. raspberries, 600 g–1 lb. 4 oz. honey.
Crush the washed and thoroughly cleaned raspberries and put them in a two-litre–4 pint jar in a cold room for 2–3 days. Then add the honey, bring to the boil, strain and pour into pre-heated bottles and close them. (300 ml–½ pint milk and the whipped white of an egg may be added to the honey, which is then to be boiled and strained, before mixing with the fruit.)

Honey Vinegar
Ingredients: 1 kg–2 lb. honey, 1 dried roll, 4 litres–7 pts water.

Pour the water and honey into a large jar, add a crumbled roll, cover with a piece of linen and put in a warm place to ferment. Fermentation will be completed in about 4 weeks, after which the jar should be tightly covered. When the liquid has cleared, pass through a tightly woven cloth and keep in well-closed bottles.

Lettuce salad with honey dressing
Ingredients: 3 lettuces, 3 hard-boiled eggs, 1 tbsp mustard, 2 tsp honey, a little salt, ground black pepper and paprika, 1 tbsp salad oil, 2 tbsp honey vinegar, 2 tbsp sour cream.
Wash the lettuces well, cut in halves (or perhaps into strips), dip them in a mild brine to which a little honey vinegar has been added and put them in the salad bowl. Cut the hard-boiled eggs into halves, scoop out the yolks, mash them with a fork, then add the mustard, honey, salt, pepper, and paprika. Stir until smooth, then add the oil, honey vinegar and sour cream. Pour over the lettuces and decorate with the rings of hard-boiled egg-whites.

Honey-and-orange butter can be made by mixing 200 g–7 oz. honey with 200 g – 7 oz. butter and adding the grated peel of one orange.

Honey cream
Cool 200 ml – ⅓ pint cream and whip in a cool place. When stiff enough add 10 g–½ oz. of castor sugar and when thoroughly mixed trickle a spoonful of cooled honey into it whipping all the time. On hot summer days the bowl for whisking may be put into a bigger bowl filled with icy water. Honey cream is delicious with coffee, cocoa, in ice creams, for decorating pastries or with fruit, especially raspberries or strawberries.

Lady in a costume of the 18th century. Carved wood. Kiscelli Museum, Budapest

Sweetening with honey
To cold and warm dishes, and pastry alike honey can be added instead of all or part of the sugar. Its handling and use are simple and the resulting pleasant and soft taste of the food is certainly worth the trouble. Below you will find a few suggestions each of which can be adapted freely according to taste.

Apples with walnut and honey
Ingredients: 2 firm apples, 2 tbsp honey, 20 g–1 oz. ground walnuts, 20 g–1 oz. washed sultanas, 10–15 g–½ oz. butter, 50 ml–1/10 pint rum.
Soak the sultanas in rum, and wash and core the apples. Mix the sultanas with the ground walnuts and honey and fill the hole in the apples with this mixture. Put the apples into a buttered, fire-proof dish and bake in a pre-heated medium oven for 15–20 minutes. Serve warm.

Honey omelette
Ingredients: 100 g–4 oz. honey, the grated peel of ½ lemon, 5 egg yolks, 60 g–2 oz. flour, 4 egg whites, 40 g–1½ oz. butter.
Mix the honey well with the grated lemon peel and the 5 egg yolks. Whisk the egg whites until firm, add the honey mixture and the melted butter, and finally add the flour gradually. Bake in a pan or cake tin.

Honey titbits for children
Ingredients: 300 g–11 oz. honey, 150 g–5 oz. chopped walnuts, 80 g–3 oz. poppyseed browned in a pot, 10 g–⅓ oz. butter.
Boil and brown the honey with a little water, so that firm balls can be formed of it. Add the butter, chopped walnuts and browned poppyseeds, mix well, spread and put on a sheet of wafer. When cool cut into pieces.

Walnut filling with honey
Ingredients: 200 g–7 oz. ground walnuts, 30 g–1 oz. fine white bread crumbs or 60 g–2 oz. grated honeycake, 100 g–4 oz. sugar, 60 g–2 oz. honey, 20 g–⅔ oz. candied orange peel chopped, 20 g–⅔ oz. sultanas, 10 g–⅓ oz. vanilla sugar or 10 g–⅓ oz. ground cinnamon, the grated peel of ½ lemon, 50 ml–1/10 pint milk.
Mix the ingredients with some water in a pot over heat then set the mixture aside for a day.

Poppyseed filling with honey
Ingredients: 200 g–7 oz. ground poppyseed, 100 g–4 oz. sugar, 60 g–2 oz. honey, 30 g–1 oz. sultanas, 40 g–1½ oz. morello cherries candied or preserved in honey, the grated peel of ½ orange, 10 g–⅓ oz. cloves, 100 ml–⅕ pt milk. Mix and warm the ingredients in a pot adding enough water to make it spreadable.

Pastry for the poppyseed and walnut fillings
Ingredients: 300 g–11 oz. flour, 120 g– 4 oz. margarine, 2 eggs, 20 g–⅔ oz. yeast, 60 g–2 oz. sugar, 20 g–⅔ oz. honey.
Mix the ingredients and knead the dough. (The yeast will act quicker if it is stirred with half of the sugar until it has liquefied.) Leave it for a night (though this is not absolutely necessary) then roll out thin and spread with one of the fillings. Roll up, brush with egg yolk, place side by side in a greased baking tin and bake.

Home-made honeycakes and other pastries made with honey

The quality and softness of the pastry will be better if honey is used instead of sugar. 1.25 kg –2½ lb. honey is to be used to replace 1 kg–2 lb. of sugar and the quantity of water or milk is to be decreased by 250 ml–½ pint at the same time.

For birthdays, Christmas, Easter or for a summer holiday our mothers baked honeycake well in advance so that it would be soft by the time we ate it.

Christmas honeycake
Ingredients: 250 g–8 oz. wheat flour, 250 g–8 oz. rye flour, 120 g–4 oz. honey, 70 g–3 oz. sugar, 60 g–2 oz. fine, smooth jam, 10 g–⅓ oz. salt volatile, 5 g–⅕ oz. pearl-ash, 4 egg yolks, 5 g–⅕ oz. each of cinnamon, cloves, mace and aniseed (the last finely pounded in a mortar).
Dissolve the salt volatile and pearl-ash separately in 1 tbsp milk each, then mix all the ingredients and leave for two days. Knead well and roll out thin on a smooth floured surface. Use a small piece for a trial baking; if the holes are too big, knead in some more flour. Cut stars, rings, pretzels, etc. from the rolled pastry with cutters, and place on a margarined baking tin. Brush them with egg yolk which may be mixed with a little sour cream either before baking or immediately after taking out of the oven. Bake for 7–8 minutes to a nice brown colour. If baked on a floured baking sheet, the little cakes may be coated with sugar frosting.

Sugar frosting
Boil 1 kg– 2 lb. sugar with 400 ml –⅔ pint water until a long thread can be drawn with your fingers from the wooden spoon dipped into the syrup. The honeycakes frosted with this mixture should be dried in the oven and then spread on a table. A Santa Claus, an Easter rabbit, an egg, or even dolls can be made from it. Cut the desired shape out of cardboard, press it on the dough and cut it out with a knife.

Ornamental pipe. Honeycake mould. Pear-wood.
Height: 19 cm. Déri Museum, Debrecen

Alföld honeycake (Honeycake from the Great Hungarian Plain)
Ingredients: 250 g–9 oz. honey, 1 tbsp rum, 5 g–1/5 oz. pearl-ash, 250 g–9 oz. flour, 2 eggs, 100 g–4 oz. finely ground hazelnut, walnut or almond kernels.
Cook the honey in a pot until light brown, then pour into the middle of the mound of flour, taking care lest it trickle down. Mix and knead together and leave until the next day. Then add the rest of the ingredients and knead well. Bake in a buttered and floured baking tin (usually a long, rectangular one is used for this recipe) until golden brown. After taking it out of the oven, brush the top of it with a mixture of water and honey and cover the rest of its surface with the frosting described above. Put back into the oven and dry. The frosting will have a marble-like pattern.

Basle honeycake
Ingredients: 300 g–11 oz. honey, 300 g–11 oz. sugar, the juice and grated peel of 1 lemon, the candied peel of 1 orange, 5 g–1/5 oz. cinnamon, 5 g–1/5 oz. nutmeg, 150 g–5 oz. finely ground almonds, 700 g–1 lb. 7 oz. wheat flour, 10 g–1/3 oz. pearl-ash, 50 ml–1/10 pt rum, 10 g–1/3 oz. salt volatile dissolved in milk, 150 ml–1/4 pt water.
Boil the honey with the sugar and water, add the spices, the juice and grated peel of the lemon, the finely chopped orange peel, flour, almonds and finally the pearl-ash. Leave it for a day, then knead well. Bake in a hot oven in a buttered and floured tin. When cool cover with sugar syrup. Serve in slices.

Chocolate honeycake
Ingredients: 150 g–5 oz. honey, 150 g–5 oz. margarine or butter, 3 eggs, 250 g–8 oz. wheat flour, 50 g–2 oz. potato flour or grits, 10 g–1/3 oz. salt volatile, the grated peel of 1/2 lemon. Ingredients for the *chocolate icing:* 70 g–2½ oz. honey, 100 ml–1/5 pint cream, 50 g–2 oz. blanched almonds, hazelnuts or walnuts, 50 g–2 oz. cocoa.
Whisk the whole eggs, melt the margarine, then mix it with the honey and add the eggs. Then

Angel with spread wings. Honeycake mould carved of hard wood. Height: 16 cm. Déri Museum, Debrecen

add the wheat flour, potato flour and salt volatile, and season with the grated lemon peel. Put into a low, round buttered (or margarined) cake-tin and bake in a medium oven for 35–40 minutes. Turn the cake out of the tin and when cool coat with the cream cooked from the honey, milk and cocoa powder. Decorate with almonds, hazelnuts or walnuts.

Spiced honeycake

Ingredients: 100 g–4 oz. margarine or butter, 100 g–4 oz. sugar, 100 g–4 oz. honey, 2 eggs, 200 g– 7 oz. flour, 10 g–⅓ oz. salt volatile, ½ tsp each of ginger, cloves and cinnamon, 50 g–2 oz. candied orange peel, some fine white bread crumbs. Choose a round or rectangular baking tin, grease it and cover thinly with the bread crumbs.

Boil the honey, cut the orange peel into squares and whisk the eggs. Now beat the butter or margarine with the sugar, then add the honey, orange peel and eggs followed by the flour, spices and salt volatile. Pour into the baking tin and bake in a medium oven for 40 minutes.

Hungarian honey-bread

Ingredients: 500 g–1 lb. wheat flour, 500 g–1 lb. boiled honey, 1 egg, 2 egg yolks, a little cinnamon and ground cloves, 5 g–⅕ oz. tartaric acid, 20 g–⅔ oz. baking soda and a little milk.

Mix and knead the ingredients well with the exception of the baking soda which is to be added last dissolved in the milk. Roll the dough out to a thickness of about 20 mm–⅘ inch, brush the top with egg yolk and bake on a buttered baking sheet. When cool it may be sliced. It will not dry out for months.

It can be made with 250 g–8 oz. wheat flour and 250 g–8 oz. rye flour instead of 500 g–1 lb. wheat flour; chopped walnuts can be sprinkled on top. The cake should be sliced just before serving.

Easy-to-make, long-lasting honeycake

Ingredients: 4 eggs, 50 g–2 oz. wheat flour, 120 g–4 oz. sugar, 50 g–2 oz. butter, 250 g–8 oz. honey, 10 g–⅓ oz. baking soda, 100 g–4 oz. chopped almonds, walnuts or hazelnuts according to taste, the grated peel and juice of 1 lemon and a little milk.

Knead the ingredients together finally adding the baking soda dissolved in the milk. After leaving for a day bake the dough in 10 cm–4 inch wide strips in a medium oven. It will keep for a long time. Slice before serving.

Hungarian honey gateau

Ingredients: 120 g–4 oz. honey, 100 g–4 oz. castor sugar, 8 eggs, 100 g–4 oz. coarsely ground wheat flour, 150 g–5 oz. blanched ground almonds or walnuts, 100 g–4 oz. grated chocolate, the juice of 1 lemon, 5 g–⅕ oz. baking soda, 500 g–1 lb. currant or other sourish jam.

Whisk the 8 egg yolks with the sugar and honey, add the almonds, chocolate and paking powder, the 8 beaten stiff egg whites, then fold in the flour gradually and finally add the lemon juice. Bake in a greased and floured cake tin for about 30 minutes in a preheated oven. When cool, cut in half horizontally and fill with the jam. It can then be covered with sugar frosting (see page 107) or with honey fondant (page 110).

Hungarian honey strudel

Ingredients: 1 package strudel sheets, 250 g–9 oz. blanched almonds pounded in a mortar, 250 g–9 oz. acacia honey, the grated peel of 1 orange and 1 lemon, 2 eggs, 4 egg yolks.

Unfold the strudel sheets on a white table-cloth, mix the ingredients for the filling, whisk the mixture and spread on the strudel sheets. Roll them up, brush with egg yolk, place side by side in a buttered baking tin and bake. Cut into pieces while warm, sprinkle with castor sugar and serve.

Honey fondant

Boil 50 g–2 oz. sugar with 200 ml–⅓ pt water in a pot until a blister can be formed on it by blowing. The blister test is to be made by dipping a thick wire loop into the thick syrup. If it fills the loop and the film of syrup can be blown away, it is to be boiled a little more. Add 10 g–4 oz. honey and test again. If it is successful, pour the mixture onto a greased marble slab or other smooth surface, taking care that it shouldn't run all over the place. Sprinkle with water and when it has cooled a bit move a knife over its surface as if you wanted to spread something on the fondant. The fondant can be flavoured with ground walnuts, rum, or cocoa, it can be re-heated and 40 g–1½ oz. butter added to it. Pour again half-melted on an oily surface and shape with a knife to the desired thickness. After a few minutes the fondant can be cut up for use as sweet Christmas tree decorations, but it can also be used for coating cakes. It is important that the brim of the pot in which the syrup is cooked is continuously wiped with vinegar diluted with water lest crystals form before the right time.

Honey candy

Ingredients: 500 g–1 lb. sugar, 200 ml–⅓ pt water, 150 g–5 oz. honey.

Heat the sugar with the water to 145° C, i.e. until the sample taken with the wooden spoon is brittle. Add the honey and continue boiling until brittle again. Pour out on a greased marble or other smooth surface. It is a good idea to prepare a frame 15 by 20 centimetres–6 inch by 8 inch and leave the mixture to cool in it. Do not wait until it gets hard but cut it up while it is still pliable, with a knife, dipped in water. Honey sweets are very good for sucking away at by either children or adult with a persistent cough.

Richly decorated scissors. Carved honeycake mould.
Déri Museum, Debrecen

Zwieback for children

Ingredients: 600 g–1 lb. 4 oz. wheat flour, 4 g–1½ oz. yeast, 150 g–5 oz. honey, 120 g–4 oz. butter, 5 g–⅕ oz. salt, 5 egg yolks, 400 ml–⅔ pint milk.

Make a leaven of 150 g–5 oz. flour and the yeast with 200 ml–⅓ pint lukewarm milk and let it rise at 28–30°C. When it has risen, mix with the rest of the ingredients, make 3 loaves of the dough, cover them with a cloth and let them rise. Make sticks, the width of 4 fingers and 2 fingers high, and bake them in a buttered baking tin until light brown. When cool, cut into a finger thick slices and brown a little in a medium oven. Some of them may be rolled in castor sugar while hot.

Popcorn with honey

Ingredients: 30 g–1 oz. honey, 20 g–⅔ oz. margarine, 1 litre–1¼ pt popcorn.

Brown the honey in a 1½ litre pot with the margarine then gradually add the popcorn. When it has absorbed the melted honey and margarine mixture, shape little balls of it. Cool and serve.

Apple meringue with honey

Ingredients: 1 kg–2 lb. apples, 2 egg whites, 200 g–7 oz. honey, the grated peel and juice of ½ lemon.

Bake the apples and pass them through a sieve. When cool, whip them in a liquidiser together with the egg whites and lemon juice. In the meantime trickle in the warmed honey. It is especially suitable for decorating and flavouring cakes but can also be served in small glass bowls.

Fruit yoghurt with honey

Ingredients: 40 g–1½ oz. honey, 1 cup of yoghurt, 100 ml–⅕ pt milk, 50 g–2 oz. well washed and strained fresh or frozen raspberries or raspberry jam diluted with raspberry squash.

Mix the honey and the yoghurt well, add the milk and the raspberries, whip in a liquidiser and serve in glasses decorated with whole raspberries.

Cheese cream with honey and apples
Ingredients: 120 g–4 oz. honey, 400 g–14 oz. grated apples, 1 egg yolk, 60 g–2 oz. chopped walnuts, a pinch of cinnamon, the peel and juice of ½ lemon, 200 g–7 oz. cottage cheese.
Cool the ingredients, with the exception of the honey, then add the lemon juice, grated lemon peel, egg yolk, cinnamon, cottage cheese, and finally the honey and mix well either by hand or with a whisk. Serve cold.

Tomato drink with honey
Ingredients: 50 g–2 oz. honey, a pinch of salt, the juice of 2 lemons, 400 ml–¾ pt tomato juice. Mix the ingredients either in a bowl by hand or in a liquidiser. Serve in glasses.

Morello-cherry liqueur with honey
Ingredients: 500 ml–1 pint small black morello-cherries, 500 ml–1 pint pure alcohol, 500 ml–1 pint acacia honey, 5 g–⅕ oz. cloves, 300 ml–½ pint soft water.
Wash and clean the morello-cherries and crush them, together with the stones. Put them into a jar, add the water and set aside for 2 days. Then add the alcohol, honey and cloves, shake well and leave for 40 days. Filter and bottle the liqueur. If it is allowed to continue maturing in bottles its taste will be more mellow.

Honey biscuits
Ingredients: 500 g–1 lb. wheat flour, a pinch of salt, 70 g–3 oz. honey, 30 g–1 oz. sugar, 10 g–⅓ oz. vanilla sugar, 120 g–4 oz. butter, 5 g–⅕ oz. salt volatile, 5 g–⅕ oz. baking soda, a few tbsps water.

Mounted hussar. Honeycake mould. Pear-wood. Kiscelli Museum, Budapest

Mix the ingredients and knead the flour into the mixture. After leaving it for 3–4 hours roll out thin cut into longish pieces and bake in a warm oven.

Dijon honeycake
Ingredients: (A) 700 g–1 lb. 4 oz. honey, 800 g–1 lb. 11 oz. flour, the grated peel of 2 lemons. (B) 3 eggs yolks, 10 g–⅓ oz. salt volatile, 10 g –⅓ oz. baking soda, a little lemon flavouring.
Knead a dough from the (A) ingredients, leave for 3 weeks then add the (B) ingredients and knead well. Make a ball of 10 g–⅓ oz. and bake it. If it is too loose, add flour to the dough, if too solid, castor sugar. Roll out a sheet which will cover the bottom of two baking tins. Bake in a medium oven for 25 minutes. Brush with a mixture of egg yolk and water before taking out. When cool, leave it in a humid place. In 3 days it will be soft and can be sliced.

Bibliography

Ambrózy, Pál: *A méz* (Honey), Budapest, 1912.

Az apiterápia ma (Apitherapy Today). Bucharest, Apimondia 1976.

Apuleius, Lucius: *Az aranyszamár* (The Golden Ass). Budapest, 1971.

Balassa M. Iván: "Méhesek a Hegyközben és a Bodrogközben" (Apiaries in the Hegyköz and Bodrogköz). *Néprajzi Értesítő,* Budapest, 1971, pp. 83–104.

Baruch, F. J.: *Naturhistorisches Bilderbuch.* Vienna, 1805.

Beliczay, László: *A méz ipari feldolgozása. Mézes sütemények* (Industrial processing of honey. Honeycakes). Műszaki Könyvkiadó, Budapest, 1960.

Beliczay, László: "A mézeskalácsos és viaszöntő ipar és a méhészek" (Bee-keepers and the honeycake and wax-taper making trades). *MTA Veszprémi Akadémiai Bizottság Értesítője,* Vol. 2, Veszprém, 1979.

Besselich, N.: *Honigkuchen und Lebkuchen.* Verlag der Konditor Zeitung, Trier, 1926.

Bessler, I. G.: *Geschichte der Bienenzucht.* Stuttgart, 1886.

Butler, Colin G.: *The World of the Honeybee.* Collins, London, 1976.

Chiflet: Anastasia Childerici regis. Anvers, 1655.

Codex diplomaticus Hungariae ecclesiasticus ac civilis. Studio et opera Georgii Fejér, Buda, 1829–44.

Comenius, Johannes Amos: *Orbis sensuarum pictus bilingvis ...* Coronae 1685, Facsimile edition. MTA–Hungarian UNESCO Committee, Budapest, 1970.

Csaplovits, János: *A méhtartásnak új-, könnyű- és hasznos módja kettős köpükben* (The New, Simplified and Practical Method of Keeping Bees in Double Skeps). Miskolc, 1816.

Dümichen, I.: *Die erste bis jetzt aufgefundene sichere Angabe über die Regierungszeit eines ägyiptischen Königs (Bichens) aus dem altern Reich.* Leipzig, 1845.

Ebers, Georg: *Das hermetische Buch der Arzneimittel der alten Egypter.* Leipzig, 1875.

Encyclopaedia Britannica. Vol. 17. London, 1974.

Engel, Johann Christian von: *Gesichte des Ungarischen Reichs.* Vienna, 1813–14.

Faluba, Zoltán: *Méz és viasz* (Honey and Wax). Budapest, 1955.

Mounted hussar. Carved of oak. Déri Museum, Debrecen

Faluba, Zoltán: *Méhek, méhészkedés* (Bees and Bee-keeping). Budapest, 1983.

Forman, Werner–Forman, Bedrich: *Aegyptische Kunst, Aus den Sammlungen des Museums in Kairo.* Prague, 1962.

Frauenfelder: "Der Honig als Genuss-, Nähr- und Kräftigungsmittel". *Schweizerische Bienenzeitung.* Zurich, 1921.

Gedde, John: *Angliai méhes kert* (Bee-gardens in England). Eger, 1768.

Gelléri, Mór: *A magyar ipar úttörői. Élet és jellemrajzok* (The Pioneers of Hungarian Industry. Biographies and Portrays of Character). Pest, 1887.

Gergelyffy, András: *"Technológia vagyis a mesterségek- és némely alkotmányok rövid leírása" (Technology: A Short Description of Trades and Products).* Pozsony, 1809.

Glatz, Jakob: *Die Bilderwelt.* Vienna, 1811.

Grimm, J.: *Deutsche Rechtsalterthümer.* Berlin, 1956.

Grimm, J.: *Weisthümer.* Vol. 3. Göttingen, 1840–42.

Gründlicher Unterrict eines löbl. wohlersahlet Lebzelter Handwerks. Hauptlade zu Neu Sohl. Besztercebánya.

Hahberg, Wolf Helmhard von: *Georgina curiosa, das ist: Umständlicher Bericht und klarer Unterricht von dem adelichen Land- und Feld-leben...* Vol. 1–2. Nuremberg, 1687.

Hajdu, Péter: *A magyarság kialakulásának előzményei* (The Antecedents of the Formation of the Hungarian People). Budapest, 1953.

Halifman, Josef Androvics: *A méhek* (Bees). Budapest, 1955.

A méhlegelő (The Bee Pasture). Ed. L. Halmágyi. Budapest, 1975.

Handerla, György: *Új méhész* (The New Bee-keeper). Pozsony, 1794.

Hansen, Hans Jürgen: *Geschichte des Backwerks.* Stalling Verlag, Oldenburg/Hamburg, 1968.

Hehn, Victor: *Kulturpflanzen und Haustiere.* Berlin, 1911.

Hérics-Tóth, Jenő–Taxner, Károly: *Szeszes italok és ecet készítése mézből* (The Preparation of Liquors and Vinegar from Honey). Budapest, 1926.

The Holy Bible... The Authorized (King James) Version, The Gideons International, Copyright 1961. The National Publishing Co. Printed in USA.

Horhi, Miklós: *Méhes emberek Tanittatása az Méh Szaporodásával* (The Experience of Bee-keepers in Bee-Rearing). (1636). Manuscript. Copy by hand 1775. National Széchényi Library location mark: Oct. Hung. 570.

Ipolyi, Arnold: *Magyar mythologia* (Hungarian Mythology). Pest, 1854.

Jakab, Mihály–Orbán, György–etc.: *A méhpempő kérdéséről* (About the Royal Jelly). Budapest, 1960.

Jarvis, DeForest Clinton: *A méz és más természetes készítmények* (Honey and Other Natural Preparations). Bucharest, 1976.

Jarvis, D. C.: *A reuma méhészeti termékekkel és természetes úton való gyógyítása* (Natural Cures for Rheumatism Using Apicultural Products). Bucharest, 1979.

Jávorka, Sándor–Csapody, Vera: *Erdő, mező virágai* (Flowers of Forests and Meadows). Budapest, 1958.

Jávorka, Sándor–Csapody, Vera: *Iconographia florae partis Austro–Orientalis Europae Centralis*. Budapest, 1975.

Jolles, Adolf: *Die Nahrungs- und Genussmittel und ihre Beurteilung*. Leipzig and Vienna, 1926.

Josephus Flavius: *A zsidó háború* (The Jewish War). Budapest, 1964.

Kádár, Lajos: *A méh és lakása* (The Bee and Its Habitat). Budapest, 1921.

Kaltenegger, Leonides: *A méz a történelemtudomány és a tapasztalat ítélőszéke előtt* (Honey Before the Tribunal of History and Experience). Losonc, 1894.

Kántor, János: *A méhekről* (Bees). Sopron, 1812.

Kerecsényi, Edit: *A népi méhészkedés története, ősformái és gyakorlata Nagykanizsa környékén* (The History, Archetypes and Practice of Bee-keeping by the People of the Nagykanizsa Area). *Néprajzi Közlemények,* Budapest, 1968.

Kietz, E. R.: *Die Honig- und Lebkuchen Fabrikation*. Killinger Verlagsgesellschaft, Nordhausen am Harz, 1938.

Kiger, J.: *Le pain d'épices. Fabrication* – Analyse. Dunod, Paris, 1948.

Knauz, Nándor–Dedek Crescens, Lajos: *Monumenta ecclesiae Strigonensis*. Vol. 1–2. Esztergom, 1874–82.

Koch: "Der Honig als Kraftquelle für das Herz." Vortrag im *Imkerkund*. Neuheim, 28th July, 1933.

Koch: "Der Honig als Nahrungs-, Heil- und Genussmittel". *Bienewirtschaftliches Zentralblatt,* 1927/66.

Kokas, V.: "Die Wirkung der Genussmittel auf die Bewegung und die Glukoseresorption." *Naunyn–Schmiedebergs Archiv* 169. 1933.

Kovács, Miklós: *Régmúlt idők méhészete* (Bee-keeping in Bygone Times). Budapest, 1959.

Lassen, Christian: *Indische Altertumskunde*. Bonn, 1849.

Lommel, Andreas: *Vorgeschichte und Naturvölker*. Vol. 1. Bertelmann Verlag, 1967.

Luptovszka–Horecna, Klotilda: *A méz felhasználása a háztartásban* (Household Uses of Honey). Bratislava, 1970.

Maeterlinck, Maurice: *A méhek élete* (The Life of the Bee). Budapest, 1912.

Magyar Gazdaságtörténeti Szemle. Budapest, 1895. Magyar méz és egyéb méhészeti termékszabványok (Hungarian Standards for Honey and other Apicultural Products). 1970–1980.

Magyar méz és egyéb méhészeti termékszabványok. 1970–1980

Magyar Néprajzi Lexikon (Hungarian Encyclopaedia of Ethnography). Ed. Gyula Ortutay. Akadémiai Kiadó, Budapest, 1980–83.

A magyarországi méhtartás rövid tudománya (The Short Science of Bee-keeping in Hungary). Vác, 1795.

Mátyus, István: *Ó és új diaetetica* (Old and New Dietetics). Pozsony, 1787–93.

Méhészet, 1975–80. (Bee-keeping, a review)

Méhészet Romániában, Bucharest, 1978.

Merlet, Pierre Yves: *Le miel. Thèse pour le doctorat vétérinaire*. Toulouse, 1981.

Móczár, László "Rovarok és a technika. *Állatvilág.*" (Insects and Technology. The Animal Kingdom.) Budapest, 1982/3.

Nagy, János: *Méhi gazdaság* (Bee Husbandry). Győr, 1786.

Nagy, János: *A méhészet múltja* (The History of Bee-keeping). Budapest, 1810.

Nagy, János: *"Tudósítás a sopronyi nádméz-fabrikának felállításáról"* (A Report of the setting-up of the Sopron Cane-sugar factory). Sopron, 1794.

Nagy, Miklósné: *A méz felhasználása a háztartásban* (Household Uses of Honey). Budapest, 1929.

Nemesszeghy, Kálmán: *A méz a háztartásban* (Honey in the Household). Budapest, 1929.

Ókori lexikon (Encyclopaedia of Antiquity). Ed. Vilmos Pecz. Budapest, 1904.

Örösi, Pál Zoltán: *Méhellenségek és a köpü állatvilága* (The Enemies of Bees and the Fauna of Skeps). Országos Méhészeti Egyesület, Budapest, 1939.

Örösi, Pál Zoltán: *Méhek között* (Among Bees). Budapest, 1968.

Paillon, Pierre: *La fabrication des produits alimen a taires su miel*. Girardot, Paris, 1960.

Pálfi, Lőrinc: *Erdélyi méhecske* (The Small Transylvanian Bee). 3rd ed, Kolozsvár, 1783.

Radio Report with Attila Bács in *Food Magazine,* about honey.

Reinhardt: "Der Wert des Bienenhonigs als Nahrungs- und Heilmittel." *Schweizerische Bienenzeitung*. Zurich, 1926.

Horse with ornamented saddle walking among flowers. Carved honeycake mould. Kiscelli Museum, Budapest

Rigó, János–Sós, Aladár: *"Jelentés az akácméz kórélettani hatásáról"* (A Report of the Pathophysiological Effects of Acacia Honey). Budapest, 1978. Manuscript.
Rodiczky, Jenő: *A magyar méhészet múltjáról* (The History of Hungarian Apiculture). Budapest, 1802.
Root, A. I.: *The ABC and XYZ of Bee Culture*. Medina, Ohio, 1972.
Rotschütz, I.: *Illustrierter Bienzuchtsbetrieb*. Weixelburg, 1892.
Rudnay, János: Méz (Honey). *Múzsák,* Budapest, 1974/4.
Saárossy–Kapeller, Ferenc: *A méhészet múltjáról és jelenlegi közigazgatásáról* (Past and Present Administration of Apiculture). Budapest, 1902.
Salamon, F.: "Gyertyás szertartások" (Candle Ceremonies). *Századok,* 1881, pp. 643–76.
Schönfeld, Antonin: *A mézelő méh anatómiája, morfológiája és fiziológiája* (The Anatomy, Morphology and Physiology of the Honeybee). Budapest, 1962.
Schulz–Knott: "Der Honiggebrauch in der Kinderernährung." *Journal Pédiatrique,* Paris, 1938/13.
Schulze, Werner: *Gewärze und sonstige Gewürzmittel*. Fachbuchverlag, Leipzig, 1950.
Shabaskov, Ivan: *Ailleurs... l'apiculture aujourd'hui en URSS*. L'Abeille de France. Paris, 1980/2.
Shakespeare, William: *The Complete Works of William Shakespeare*. Ed. W. J. Craig. London, Oxford University Press, New York, Toronto, 1962.
Sperling–Caron: "The movable-comb frameless hive." *American Bee Journal,* New York, 1980/4.
Spöttel, Walter: *Honig und Trockenmilch. Biochemie und therapeutische Bedeutung*. Ambrosius Verlag, Leipzig, 1950.
Stegman, J. H.: *Der Pfefferkuchenbäcker und Lebküchler*. Leipzig, 1923.
Stitz, János: *A méz* (Honey). Pécs, 1934.
Studia Comitantendia. Tanulmányok Pest megye múzeumaiból (Studies from the Museums of Pest County). Szentendre, 1975.
Szabadfalvi, József: *"A magyar mézeskalácsosság kialakulásának kérdéséhez"* (The Development of Honeycake Making in Hungary). Debrecen, 1909.
Szabadfalvi, József: "A magyar mézeskészítés" (Meadmaking in Hungary). *Műveltség és hagyomány* (Education and Tradition). Tankönyvkiadó, Budapest, 1961.
Szentkuthy, Miklós: *II. Silvester második élete* (The Second Life of Sylvester II). Budapest, 1972.
Szilágyi, Miklós: "Adatok a Nagykunság XVIII. századi néprajzához. Méhészet a Nagykunságban a XVIII. század második felében". (Data for the Eighteenth Century Ethnography of the Nagykunság. Bee-keeping in the Nagykunság in the Second Half of the Eighteenth Century). *Szolnok megyei múzeumi adattár.* Szolnok, 1966.
Szondy György Album (György Szondy Album). Ed. and published by Lajos Pongrácz. Esztergom–Ipolyság, 1885.
Telegdy Kováts, László: *Élelmiszerkémia és élelmezési iparok* (Food Chemistry and the Food Processing Industries). Budapest, 1951.
Tonelli, Sándor: *Száz év előtt. 1842. Az Országos Iparegyesület alapításának esztendeje*. (One Hundred Years Ago. 1842. The Year of the Foundation of the National Industrial Association). Budapest, 1942.
Traxler, Hans: *Die Wahrheit über Hansel und Gretel*. Frankfurt am Main, 1978.
Veszelszky, Antal: *Házi orvosságok* (Home Medicine). Vác, 1808.
Weber, J. M. Erich: *Webers billiger Fechunterricht ... Konditorei*. Radebeul–Dresden, 1938.
Weiner, Piroska: *Carved Honeycake Moulds*. Budapest, 1981.
Wenczel, Gusztáv: *Árpádkori új okmánytár* (A New Collection of Documents from the Age of the Árpáds). Vol. 1–12. Pest, 1860–74.
Yuskin, John: *Pure, White and Deadly*. London, 1972.
Zaiss, R.: "Der Honig als Volksgesundheitsmittel." *Homöopatisches Monatsblatt,* 1932.
Zimányi, Lajos: *"Élelmiszerek áruismerete"* (Description of Commercial Foodstuffs). Főiskolai jegyzet (Lecture Notes). Budapest, 1971.

Honeycake mould. Height: 37 cm. Déri Museum, Debrecen
Dress sword, its hilt forming a bird's head and its blade ornamented with floral design and the Hungarian coat of arms with the crown.

ISBN 963 13 2256 4

Printed in Hungary, 1987
Kner Printing House, Békéscsaba